REBEL LAWYER

WAYNE COLLINS AND THE DEFENSE OF JAPANESE AMERICAN RIGHTS

CHARLES WOLLENBERG

Heyday, Berkeley, California
California Historical Society, San Francisco, California

Library of Congress Cataloging-in-Publication Data

Names: Wollenberg, Charles, author.
Title: Rebel lawyer : Wayne Collins and the defense of Japanese American rights / Charles Wollenberg.
Description: Berkeley, California : Heyday, 2018. | Includes bibliographical references.
Identifiers: LCCN 2017058739 (print) | LCCN 2017058803 (ebook) | ISBN 9781597144391 (E-pub) | ISBN 9781597144360 (hardcover : alk. paper)
Subjects: LCSH: Collins, Wayne (Wayne Mortimer), 1899- | Lawyers--United States--Biography. | Japanese Americans--Civil rights. | World War, 1939-1945--Japanese Americans. | Japanese Americans--Legal status, laws, etc.
Classification: LCC KF373.C635 (ebook) | LCC KF373.C635 W65 2018 (print) | DDC 341.6/70973--dc23
LC record available at https://lccn.loc.gov/2017058739

Cover Art: Wayne Collins with Iva Toguri, 1949. Barney Peterson, *San Francisco Chronicle*, Polaris.

Book Design: Ashley Ingram

Orders, inquiries, and correspondence should be addressed to:
Heyday
P.O. Box 9145, Berkeley, CA 94709
(510) 549-3564, Fax (510) 549-1889
www.heydaybooks.com

Printed in Saline, MI, by McNaughton and Gunn

10 9 8 7 6 5 4 3 2 1

CONTENTS

PREFACE

When I was a graduate student at UC Berkeley many years ago, my professors warned me against "present-minded history," historical writing that imposed the standards and values of the present upon the past. The professors argued that you had to accept and understand the past on its own terms, rather than through the lens of present-day morality. (Even then, I wondered how you would practice that principle when writing a history of Nazi Germany.)

In this study of Wayne Collins and his defense of Japanese American rights, however, I found that present-minded history was not the problem. Instead, it seemed that Collins's standards and values and the issues he was confronting in the 1940s were dominating the political and social landscape of the second decade of the twenty-first century. I began my research while Donald Trump's presidential campaign was appealing to a wave of nativism and anti-immigrant feeling. While I was writing the manuscript, lawyers objecting to President Trump's executive order banning certain Muslim immigrants were using many of the same arguments that Collins had used to oppose President Franklin D. Roosevelt's executive order authorizing the removal and imprisonment of Japanese Americans. Writing about Collins left me considering a history-minded present rather than a present-minded history. One friend recently asked me where was Wayne Collins when we really needed him?

This book is not a full biography of Wayne Collins. While it covers some aspects of his personal life, it gives little attention to his private law practice and other business ventures. Instead, the book concentrates on Collins's legal fights for Nikkei rights, and it attempts to put these legal battles into the context of the larger history of Roosevelt's Executive Order 9066 and the policies it promoted. My argument is that the United States Constitution is not self-starting; it needs human intervention to transform its noble words and principles into concrete reality. It takes a particular combination of moral commitment, political conscience, and downright stubborn rebelliousness to intervene on the side of individual constitutional rights in times of national crisis, such as war. Collins had that combination of personality and character. He was hardly a flawless human being, but he was a fearless defender of the nation's most important constitutional principles. Many of those principles are under attack today, making Collins's legal efforts in defense of civil rights and civil liberties all too relevant in the twenty-first century.

I had a lot of help learning about Wayne Collins's life and times. In particular, his son, Wayne Merrill Collins, generously answered questions about his father's family and professional life. I had access to the vast collection of the Wayne M. Collins Papers at The Bancroft Library on the UC Berkeley campus, as well as sources at other branches of the university library. The archives of the Northern California branch of the American Civil Liberties Union at the California Historical Society was another valuable resource. I also used materials from the San Francisco Public Library and the

Special Collections of the UC Davis Library. I am grateful for the immense good work and dedication of the librarians and archivists at all these institutions.

Kathy, Leah, and Mike Wollenberg, along with Stan Yogi, Patricia Wakida, Jerry Herman, Tom Wolf, and Martha Bridegam read the manuscript and gave important criticisms and suggestions. I had valuable conversations with Anthea Hartig, Alison Moore, and John Tateishi, as well as feedback from Elaine Elinson, and a session at the National Japanese American Historical Society.

Finally, I am grateful to Heyday, its publisher Steve Wasserman, and especially for the support and assistance of its editorial director, Gayle Wattawa. I greatly benefited from the careful work and good advice of my Heyday editor, Briony Everroad. The book received the 2017 California Historical Society Book Award. The award is a tribute to the importance of Wayne Collins's historic fight for justice and its relevance to California and the nation, both past and present.

CHAPTER 1

9066

Although Hiroshi Kashiwagi was only twenty-two years old at the time, he says that he was already "at the low point of my life" when he met Wayne Collins in the summer of 1945. A native of the Sacramento Valley, Kashiwagi had spent three years confined at the Tule Lake Segregation Center in northeastern California. Earlier in 1945, he had made "a terrible mistake," joining five thousand other Tule Lake inmates in renouncing their American citizenship. He said he had been "a victim of the government's manipulation, of the hysteria within the camp, of the confusion in our family, and of my own stupid inertia." Now the government classified him as a "native American alien" subject to deportation to Japan, a nation he had never even visited. All that stood between Hiroshi Kashiwagi and involuntary exile was Wayne Mortimer Collins, "a small wiry looking man with short gray hair and bright sharp eyes." Kashiwagi could not believe "that this very Caucasian man, a refined, intense civil rights attorney from San Francisco, smoking incessantly, was actually on our side, outraged at our miserable situation."

What brought Kashiwagi and Collins together was Executive Order 9066, issued by President Roosevelt in February 1942, about three months after the Japanese attack on Pearl Harbor. The executive order authorized the army to remove all people of

Japanese descent from the West Coast of the United States. One hundred and twenty thousand individuals were affected, men and women, adults and children, Issei (first-generation immigrants prohibited by law from becoming American citizens), Nisei (second-generation Japanese Americans who were US citizens by virtue of their American birth), and a very few Sansei (third-generation citizens of Japanese descent). The evacuation even applied to Japanese American infants in West Coast orphanages. The government first housed the Nikkei (all people of Japanese descent), in crude temporary assembly centers and then in ten somewhat more elaborate camps, including Kashiwagi's Tule Lake Segregation Center.

Most historians of the World War II Japanese American incarceration have assumed that since the 1980s there has been a national consensus that Executive Order 9066 had been at best a mistake and at worst a serious violation of human rights and civil liberties. But in late 2015, some public figures, including Mayor David Bowers of Roanoke, Virginia, and Republican presidential candidate Donald Trump, referred to Roosevelt's action as a positive precedent for proposals to ban Syrian refugees or all Muslim immigrants from the United States. After Trump's election, Carl Higbie, described by the *New York Times* as the president-elect's "prominent surrogate," referred to Executive Order 9066 as precedent for a proposed national registry of all Muslims. The argument seemed to be that if Roosevelt as commander in chief could forcibly evacuate and imprison an entire ethnic group, then a contemporary president, perhaps a President Trump, had the power to protect the homeland by measures such as immigration bans and national registries based on religious and national identity. Seventy-three years after its proclamation, Executive Order 9066 was again relevant.

As William Faulkner once observed, "The past isn't dead. It's not even past."

By invoking Roosevelt's executive order, Bowers, Trump, and their supporters were reopening a sad chapter in American and particularly California history. While the evacuation affected parts of Washington, Oregon, and Arizona, a significant majority of those removed and incarcerated were California residents like Hiroshi Kashiwagi. California had been a center of anti-Asian prejudice since the gold rush had produced the first significant Asian immigration to the United States. By the end of the 1850s, discrimination against Chinese immigrants was already a staple of California life and politics. Congressional approval of the Chinese Exclusion Act of 1882, the first significant federal immigration restriction in American history, was a reflection of the national power and influence of the anti-Chinese movement in California and other western states. As a result of Chinese exclusion, employers in California and neighboring states were forced to turn to Japan as a new source of Asian immigrant labor. And by the beginning of the twentieth century, Japanese immigrants were the new target of the anti-Asian movement.

Prejudice against Japanese people in the early twentieth century was part of an interactive process that included the growing political rivalry between Japan and the United States in the Pacific. Acts of discrimination in the United States strengthened support for militarist and chauvinist politicians in Japan. Japanese military aggression in Asia seemed to give credence to the arguments of anti-Asian activists and "Yellow Peril" advocates in the United States. In 1906, the decision to segregate Japanese students in San Francisco public schools created a diplomatic crisis between the two countries. President Theodore Roosevelt eventually persuaded San Francisco authorities to cancel the segregation policy, but President Woodrow Wilson was unable to prevent the California legislature from passing the 1913 Alien Land Law, designed to prevent Japanese immigrants from owning land in the state. In the early 1920s, new American immigration laws extended the Chinese exclusion policy to Japan and the rest of Asia, cutting off further Japanese immigration. Because of the new restrictions, by the time of Executive Order 9066 in 1942, the majority of Nikkei affected by the evacuation were second-generation Japanese Americans and thus United States citizens.

The executive order, then, was only in part a reaction to the Japanese attack on Pearl Harbor. It was also a reflection of the long heritage of anti-Asian and particularly anti-Japanese sentiment in California and the other West Coast states that were home to virtually all Nikkei living on the American mainland. During the war, authorities interned some, but by no means all, German and Italian immigrants, and no German or Italian Americans were imprisoned without due process. In Hawai'i, where people of Japanese descent made up a third of the population, as opposed to about 1 percent in California, there was no general evacuation or incarceration, though authorities did intern a small number of Nikkei. Clearly the rules for people of Japanese descent living on the West Coast were very different than for people of various enemy nationalities living elsewhere in the United States.

The evacuation and incarceration policy was popular on the West Coast. California's congressional delegation unanimously supported it, as did liberal Democratic governor Culbert Olson. The state's leading Republican politician, state attorney general and soon-to-be governor Earl Warren, was a particularly strong defender of Nikkei removal. The California Federation of Labor, the state Chamber of Commerce, the California Farm Bureau Federation, the Native Sons and Daughters of the Golden West, and the American Legion were just some of the organizations that supported the president's action. Most California and western newspapers were on board; the *Los Angeles Times* and the publications of the Hearst and McClatchy media chains were especially vehement in their advocacy of Nikkei removal.

There was some vocal opposition to the evacuation, including from the Nikkei victims themselves. But people of Japanese descent were a tiny minority of the West Coast population; they desperately needed support from members of the white majority. A few whites did speak up, including the Berkeley-based Fair Play Committee. However, the most committed, consistent, and effective defender of the rights and liberties of the West Coast's Japanese American population was Wayne Collins.

Collins had already been involved in a number of cases related to Nikkei rights when he met Tule Lake inmate Hiroshi Kashiwagi in 1945. Collins's first Nikkei case was in defense of Fred Korematsu, who was arrested in 1942 for refusing to obey the original evacuation order. On behalf of the Northern California branch of the American Civil Liberties Union, Collins used the *Korematsu* case to challenge the constitutionality of Executive Order 9066 all the way to the US Supreme Court. Collins also represented the Tule Lake "troublemakers" who were thrown into the camp stockade without due process, and he defended the rights of more than three hundred Japanese Peruvians interned in the United States. He went on to defend Los Angeles–born Iva Toguri D'Aquino, aka Tokyo Rose, who faced treason charges for allegedly making Japanese propaganda broadcasts aimed at American servicemen in the Pacific. Most remarkably, he waged a twenty-three-year-long legal battle to defend the citizenship rights of the five thousand Tule Lake "renunciants," including Hiroshi Kashiwagi. Through all of this, Wayne Collins also maintained a general law practice that included representing victims of anticommunist loyalty oaths in the 1950s and Berkeley student activists in the 1960s.

Collins certainly did not fight all these legal battles alone. He depended on the constant support of his friend and colleague Ernest Besig, executive director of the ACLU's Northern California branch. He shared the burden of the "Tokyo Rose" defense with fellow attorneys Theodore Tamba and George Olshausen. Given the complexity of the Nikkei cases, Collins's small, one-man office would have collapsed without the work of a dedicated staff, including secretary and longtime family friend Chiyo Wada. He also depended on a dedicated group of Nisei volunteers to handle the huge volume of paperwork generated by the Tule Lake cases. And for more than a decade, Collins worked closely with the Tule Lake Defense Committee, made up of Japanese American renunciants and their families and friends. The committee's de facto executive secretary, Tetsujiro "Tex" Nakamura, became an indispensable ally and colleague.

Collins was not so much a savior as an enabler of incarcerated Japanese Americans. He fought important battles that gave like-minded people of Japanese descent the time, opportunity, and the legal and moral foundation on which to construct their own powerful campaigns for redress. And in the process, Collins had the courage to challenge directly the executive authority of the commander in chief, an immensely popular and powerful president of the United States, during time of war.

Collins had several longtime friends and many supporters, but he also had plenty of critics and enemies. He had a volatile temper and a sense of righteous morality that sometimes alienated even his closest allies. Although he was involved with the Northern California branch of the ACLU in San Francisco from its founding until his death, for decades he held a grudge against the national ACLU leadership and its New York office for actions that he believed compromised the defense of basic Nikkei rights and liberties. And he had similar profound differences with the leaders of the Japanese American Citizens League.

Yet not even Collins's most severe critics could question his commitment to the constitutional rights and personal dignity of his clients. Eight years after his death, the 1982 report of the Federal Commission on Wartime Relocation and Internment of Civilians finally concluded that Executive Order 9066 had been an unnecessary and unconstitutional exercise of presidential power. Wayne Collins had first argued that position forty years earlier, in his initial legal brief in the 1942 *Korematsu* case.

Hiroshi Kashiwagi was one of many Nikkei who benefited from the legal battles fought and won by Wayne Collins. After recovering his American citizenship in the 1950s, Kashiwagi went on to become a distinguished writer, librarian, actor, playwright, and activist. He was still going strong in 2017 at the age of ninety-five. In the fall of 2015 he appeared in San Francisco's Japantown with a number of prominent American Muslims and Japanese Americans to speak out against anti-Muslim prejudice and the terrible precedent of Executive Order 9066. At another public event that fall, responding to a question from the audience about Wayne Collins, Kashiwagi commented that one of his few regrets was that he hadn't named one of his children Wayne, after the lawyer who had been so important to the fate of the Kashiwagi family. Ten years earlier, in 2005, Hiroshi Kashiwagi had dedicated his memoir to "the memory of Wayne M. Collins who rescued me as an American and restored my faith in America."

CHAPTER 2

REBEL

Wayne Mortimer Collins was born in Sacramento in 1899. His Irish American parents, Harry and Martha Collins, had moved west from Saint Paul, Minnesota, after their first two children (one also named Wayne) died in infancy. The Collinses had better luck in Sacramento; the second Wayne and his younger brother, Leonard, survived and lived on to adulthood. The family moved to San Francisco when the brothers were still infants. Harry worked as an Associated Press telegrapher and was one of the first reporters to inform the world of the 1906 earthquake and fire. But when Harry died of tuberculosis in 1907, the family was shattered. Because of financial or emotional problems, Martha Collins could not keep custody of her boys.

The family breakup had to have been a traumatic experience for seven-year-old Wayne. It may have contributed to the difficulties he had with personal and family relationships for the rest of his life. And it may have also endowed him with the sympathy for the underdog and resistance to authority that became so much a part of his character. As an adult, Collins was not so much a political radical as a personal rebel. To some degree, his dogged, uncompromising defense of Nikkei rights must have had its origins in his unconventional childhood.

Wayne spent much of his youth at the Rock, an institutional home for poor and troubled boys located on San Francisco's Potrero Hill. The Rock was affiliated with San Francisco's Swedenborgian Church, one of several institutions in Europe and North America dedicated to the philosophy of the eighteenth-century Swedish scientist and Christian theologian, Emanuel Swedenborg. Swedenborg argued that religious belief should be based on a process of intellectual questioning and that faith alone was not enough to transform a person from "a material to a spiritual being." Faith had to be combined with charity and responsible moral conduct. Good and virtuous deeds were as important as belief. The Rock, devoted to the service of poor and troubled youth, was an institutional expression of Swedenborgian theology. Joseph Worcester, founding minister of the San Francisco church, was chairman of the Rock's governing board, which also included Bruce Porter, a fellow Swedenborgian and a well-known San Francisco landscape architect, artist, and writer.

Collins's childhood at the Rock began a lifelong connection with San Francisco's Swedenborgian community. His marriage and funeral took place in the landmark Lyon Street church that has served as San Francisco's Swedenborgian center for more than 120 years. In the 1950s he volunteered his legal services to the church and contributed funds for the establishment of Swedenborgian missions in Japan and South Africa. Throughout his adult life, Collins was a serious reader, including books on Swedenborgian theology and philosophy. Collins's commitment to the protection of civil rights and liberties was consistent with his understanding of Swedenborgian principles.

As a boy Collins formed a friendship with Rock board member

Bruce Porter, who may have served as something of a surrogate father figure. The friendship lasted until the older man's death in the 1950s. Porter supported Collins's defense of the Nikkei and his other civil rights activities. Collins served as the Porter family lawyer and eventually handled the probate process for the estates of both Bruce Porter and his wife Margaret.

It was most likely Bruce Porter who introduced the twelve-year-old Collins to Senri Nao, a prominent San Francisco Asian art dealer. A Japanese immigrant, Nao had a shop in Chinatown and cultivated relationships with San Francisco artists and collectors. The friendship with Nao, perhaps another father figure, exposed Collins to Japanese art and culture, as well as giving him his first experience with Nikkei life in America. It may have insulated him from the anti-Asian prejudice that so permeated California life. As an adult, Collins was Nao's attorney and represented him in various legal disputes. Collins also hired Nao's daughter, Chiyo Nao Wada, as his secretary. When Senri Nao died in 1967, Collins mourned him as his oldest friend, someone he had known "since I was a boy in knickerbockers."

While still living at the Rock, Collins attended what is now called Lick-Wilmerding High School, then located in San Francisco's Mission District. (The institution has gone by several different names over the years.) A private school founded by philanthropists, it offered free education to poor and working-class children. The curriculum combined academic subjects with vocational education, in effect preparing students for working-class occupations. At the school, Collins earned a reputation as something of a free-spirited rebel. His school nickname was Trotsky, apparently referring to his general rebellious nature rather than his political beliefs. A wild stunt involving the use of hydrogen sulfide resulted in his expulsion near the end of his senior year. Nevertheless, the institution eventually mailed him a diploma.

By the time Collins left high school, the United States had entered World War I. In 1918 Collins enlisted in the navy, serving in both the Atlantic and Pacific. He ended the war as a pharmacist's mate on a hospital ship transporting wounded servicemen back to the United States from Europe. He considered jumping ship and staying in France, but returned to the United States and mustered out of the navy on November 1, 1919. According to his discharge papers, the nearly twenty-year-old Collins was 5 feet, 7 inches tall, weighed 130 pounds, and had brown eyes and brown hair. During the next few years, Collins worked at several jobs, including selling encyclopedias and shoveling ice into refrigerator cars at the Pacific Fruit Express rail yards in San Francisco. But he was not satisfied with a blue-collar, working-class existence. He signed up for accounting classes but soon dropped out because the subject bored him.

In 1923 Collins enrolled at the San Francisco Law School, setting out on a path that was to lead to his life's work. The school was a private institution that provided a relatively inexpensive legal education to a working-class clientele. Most classes were held at night so that students could continue to hold day jobs. While San Francisco Law School didn't offer academic degrees, completing the four-year curriculum qualified students for the California Bar Exam and entrance into the legal profession. Collins seems to have thrived at the institution, serving as editor of the school newspaper, *The Barrister*. He also wrote articles publicizing school events for both the *San Francisco Chronicle* and the *San Francisco Examiner*.

Future California governor Edmund G. "Pat" Brown was one of his classmates. Brown started his political career early, successfully running for election as student body president. More than thirty years later, Collins was on the executive board of the San Francisco Lawyers for Brown, a campaign organization supporting the liberal Democrat in his successful 1958 race for governor.

Probably the best friend Collins made at law school was Astaroth Haskell, who eventually became the chief clerk of the California Supreme Court. Haskell was more than a decade older than Collins, but the two had common interests and ambitions. Haskell had a radical family background and may have influenced Collins's political consciousness. Haskell's father, Burnette, founded the Coast Seamen's Union, the first organization of maritime workers in California. In 1885 the elder Haskell established the Kaweah Colony, a utopian socialist lumber community located in what is now Sequoia National Park. Although the colony ultimately failed, Astaroth spent part of his childhood there. As was the case with many of his old friends, Collins eventually handled the probate proceedings for Astaroth Haskell's estate after his death in the 1950s.

On June 16, 1927, Pat Brown, Astaroth Haskell, and Wayne Collins were among the thirty members of the San Francisco Law School's graduating class (which included three women). Collins passed the bar exam that fall, and by the beginning of 1928 had opened a law office in the Mills Building on Montgomery Street in San Francisco. Although he eventually moved into the Mills Tower, a new addition to the building, Collins's office remained in the Mills complex for the rest of his life. He operated a single-lawyer firm, providing a wide range of practical legal services to individuals and

small businesses. Though he never had formal partners, he sometimes took cases in association with other attorneys with offices
in the Mills Building. One of his earliest colleagues and mentors
was Austin Lewis, whose office was across the hall from Collins's.
Lewis was another link to California's radical political past. Fifteen years before he met Collins, Lewis had defended the IWW
activists arrested in the infamous Wheatland farm workers' strike of
1913. Lewis later joined Collins and other radicals and reformers in
establishing the Northern California branch of the ACLU.

Collins was never a member of San Francisco's legal establishment, a group of well-connected wealthy attorneys who were grad-
uates of prestigious law schools. But Collins's private practice was
reasonably successful, and by 1930 he was earning enough money
to reunite his family. Probably for the first time in two decades, he
shared an apartment with his mother Martha and brother Leonard.
Martha was not working, and Leonard had recently been wiped
out by the 1929 stock market crash; so Wayne was the family's sole
breadwinner. He continued to support his mother and often his
brother for the rest of their lives. Collins was not particularly close
to Leonard, but the younger brother seemed to have an irresistible
attraction to failed business ventures and was frequently in need of
funds. In 1962, for example, Leonard, then living in Los Angeles,
asked for "another $500." Collins sent the check but wrote, "This
is the last loan you can expect from me." In fact it wasn't. Perhaps
Collins's Swedenborgian code obliged him to assist even irresponsible family members in need. After Leonard's death from cancer in
1965, Collins sent occasional checks to his brother's widow, Betty.

In 1933 Collins started a family of his own, marrying Thelma
May Garrison, an attractive woman six years his junior. She was

a graduate of Oakland Technical High School and had attended the University of California. Prior to her marriage, she worked as a secretary at a San Francisco insurance firm. Some of her family objected to her marrying a man of working-class background, but the marriage seems to have been a happy union. Like many Depression families, the couple delayed having children. Eventually, Margaret Ellen was born in 1942 and Wayne Merrill in 1945.

The Collinses lived in an apartment on the side of Nob Hill for several years but in 1950 moved to a house they purchased on Presidio Avenue on the western edge of the prosperous Pacific Heights neighborhood, just a few blocks from the Swedenborgian church. But normal family life was disrupted when Thelma was diagnosed with cancer. Collins never fully recovered from her death in 1953. He spent twenty years with Thelma, and it was the longest period of relatively happy family life Collins experienced. He never remarried.

After their mother's death, Margaret and Wayne Merrill stayed for a time at the home of William Weiner, the Collins's family doctor and close friend. The children eventually returned to the Presidio Avenue house, living there with their father and a series of housekeepers. Collins was a dutiful, if sometimes distant father. He kept Margaret's class pictures, report cards, and the programs of her synchronized swimming performances. When she attended college in Colorado and then moved to New York State with her new husband, Collins kept up a regular correspondence. Usually the letters were about practical matters—finances, living arrangements, and travel plans. But in a draft letter to Margaret's fiancé written in 1968, Collins said he had "a jewel of a daughter" and was going to acquire "a gem of a son in law."

In that same draft letter, Collins claimed he could not add his son to the list of family jewels "as he yet has to prove himself to me—which he could do if he would get a haircut and on rare occasions present a faint suggestion of respectability and be less irresponsible." Fortunately, Collins left this sentence out of the actual letter sent to Margaret's future husband, but the written outburst obviously reflected tensions between father and son. Wayne Merrill attended UC Berkeley during the mid-sixties and fully participated in the political and lifestyle rebellions of the day. However much the elder Collins was concerned about haircuts, respectability, and irresponsibility, he supported the 1964 Berkeley Free Speech Movement and served as the attorney for Mario Savio and other FSM student leaders charged with violations of university policy. When Wayne Merrill faced similar charges in 1966, as a result of his on-campus antiwar activity, his father wrote a characteristically long and spirited legal brief in defense of his son.

Wayne Merrill eventually followed in his father's professional footsteps, entering Golden Gate University School of Law in San Francisco. Wayne senior kept a copy of his son's successful 1973 application to the California Bar. Among those listed as witnesses of Wayne Merrill's good character were Dr. Weiner and other longtime Collins family associates. A year before the elder Collins's death in 1974, there seems to have been, at the very least, a cessation of hostilities between father and son.

It was in 1934, just a year after his wedding, that Wayne Mortimer Collins helped establish the Northern California branch of the American Civil Liberties Union in San Francisco, a move that would eventually lead to his participation in the Nikkei cases. Roger Baldwin founded the ACLU in New York in 1920 in response to government repression of radicals during World War I and the subsequent Red Scare. The organization was committed to protecting civil liberties, particularly free speech, against threats from both public and private entities. The national headquarters remained in New York, but the organization spawned local branches in many cities around the country. One of the early affiliates was the Southern California branch, founded in Los Angeles in 1923 by writer and activist Upton Sinclair.

Collins and other Bay Area progressives began the Northern California branch in reaction to the campaigns of corporate employers, and their conservative allies, against workers and unions. In rural California, growers and law enforcement officials used the state's criminal syndicalist law to crush strikes and jail Communist Party labor organizers. In San Francisco the 1934 maritime workers' strike led to the police killing of two union supporters and a brief but effective general strike. Though the maritime workers eventually won a substantial victory, repression of union activity, often involving serious violations of civil liberties, continued in both rural and urban California.

In 1935, the national ACLU sent Ernest Besig up to San Francisco to help establish the new branch, and that was when Besig and Collins first met. Besig was raised in a Jewish household in Boston and earned a law degree from Cornell. Committed to social change, he originally came west to work on behalf of California farm workers. For a time, he served on the staff of a Pasadena settlement house. Arriving in San Francisco in 1935, he intended to devote just thirty days to organizing the branch before returning to Southern California. He ended up staying for more than thirty years, serving as the organization's executive director until his retirement in 1971. During those years, Ernest Besig was the heart and soul of the Northern California branch and a major figure in San Francisco's progressive political community.

In spite of his law degree, Besig never joined the California Bar, depending on volunteer attorneys to represent branch clients for little or no pay. Wayne Collins was often the lawyer of choice, eventually serving as the branch's unpaid general counsel as well as a member of the governing board. Besig was described as "stubborn and intransigent" and "extremely effective at standing up for the underdog." Much the same could be said of Collins. Their friendship lasted until the 1960s, when a dispute over the disposition of a monetary bequest resulted in a serious breach. Given their difficult personalities, it's probably remarkable that the friendship lasted as long as it did.

Collins's first major case for the Northern California branch was on behalf of nine-year-old Charlotte Gabrielli, a Jehovah's Witness. In 1936 a Sacramento public school suspended Charlotte for refusing on religious grounds to recite the Pledge of Allegiance. Appearing before a Sacramento County Superior Court judge, Collins argued that her suspension was an unconstitutional violation of the First Amendment. But he also pointed out that Hitler was putting Jehovah's Witnesses in concentration camps for not swearing allegiance to the German government. Collins was often criticized for introducing such nonlegal issues into his cases, but the criticisms had little effect. Highly emotional rhetorical flourishes became a staple of Collins's legal briefs. He won the 1936 Gabrielli case at the superior and appeals court levels, but the California Supreme Court reversed the decision and allowed the school district to continue the suspension. Not until 1943, when the US

Supreme Court ruled in favor of Jehovah's Witnesses in a separate case, was Collins's position established as law.

From its beginnings in 1934–35, the Northern California branch was often in conflict with the ACLU national office. This may have been the result of dealing with the feisty personalities of rebels like Besig and Collins. But there were significant differences between the social and cultural conditions in San Francisco and New York that affected the perspectives of the national office and the Northern California branch. While there was plenty of class conflict and political repression in 1930s New York, there was nothing equivalent to the battles between labor and capital in California fields or the 1934 General Strike. And from the gold rush on, San Francisco thought of itself as a center of urban power, culture, and politics not necessarily dependent on leadership from New York and the East Coast. The Northern California branch expected to operate according to its own procedures and to determine and pursue its legal cases according to its own priorities. The New York office saw this attitude as a potential challenge to national ACLU policies and a possible threat to the image and influence of the national organization.

The participation of the Communist Party in the ACLU was one matter of conflict between San Francisco and New York. During the Depression, the party was influential in left wing politics in both cities. In the mid-thirties, communists pursued a "popular front" policy of working with other progressive groups including the ACLU. The national ACLU welcomed this cooperation, and elected party members to the organization's governing board. Local affiliates were expected to do likewise, but the Northern California branch dissented. Besig argued that party members would insist on a political litmus test for cases, defending only progressive causes. Later in life, Collins explained that like Besig, he was a First Amendment fundamentalist; he would uphold the free speech rights of conservatives and fascists as well as radicals and communists.

After the 1939 Hitler-Stalin pact establishing a temporary German-Soviet alliance, the national ACLU leadership reversed its position and expelled Communist Party member Elizabeth Gurley Flynn from the union's governing board on the grounds that she was a member of a "totalitarian organization." Ironically, the Northern California branch joined with several other ACLU affiliates in condemning the expulsion. For people like Collins and Besig, opposition to some Communist Party activities did not mean opposition to communists' constitutional rights. In the 1950s, Collins defended the civil liberties of teachers and professors, presumably including some party members, who had been fired by public colleges and school districts for not signing the State of California's anticommunist Levering Oath. He also protested the execution of Julius and Ethel Rosenberg for allegedly passing atomic secrets to the Soviet Union.

In the early years of the Northern California branch's existence, the greatest lever the national ACLU board had over the San Francisco rebels was the power of the purse. The branch needed financial assistance from the national office to support its operations and litigate its cases. To achieve autonomy from the national office, Besig worked hard to build an independent financial base. By the end of 1939, he had largely succeeded. The branch had more than six hundred dues-paying members and several patrons who gave substantial contributions. Over the next two years, the economic foundation expanded. While money was always a concern, the San Francisco office was essentially financially independent. By 1942 the rebellious Northern California branch was prepared for what was to become its most important conflict with the New York office: a battle over whether to proceed with the *Korematsu* case and Wayne Collins's constitutional challenge of Executive Order 9066.

CHAPTER 3

KOREMATSU

Wayne Collins waged a legal war against President Roosevelt's policy of removal and incarceration in the case of *Korematsu v. United States*. It was the most important legal proceeding regarding the rights of Japanese Americans on the West Coast. Collins challenged not just the constitutionality of Executive Order 9066, but Public Proclamation Nos. 1 and 2 and Civilian Exclusion Order No. 34, the implementation decrees issued by General John L. DeWitt, chief of the Western Defense Command. Collins also challenged Public Law 503, which made failure to obey the above orders and decrees a federal crime. In the process, Collins touched off an internal dispute within the ACLU that was to divide the organization for more than a quarter century. *Korematsu v. United States* pitted both Fred Korematsu against the US government and the Northern California branch of the ACLU against the organization's national leadership.

Historians and legal scholars have studied and analyzed the *Korematsu* case for seventy years. Probably the most influential work has been Peter Irons's *Justice at War*, published in 1983. Irons was an attorney and political scientist at UC San Diego. Along with Nisei researcher Aiko Herzig-Yoshinaga, he discovered substantial misconduct on the part of Department of Justice lawyers, and that discovery eventually resulted in the reversal of Fred Korematsu's conviction more than forty years after the fact. But government attorneys weren't Irons's only target; he also criticized Wayne Collins's tactics and performance. Irons described Collins as "a young San Francisco lawyer" with a "marginal" legal practice. In fact, by the beginning of the *Korematsu* case, Collins was in his forties and had been practicing law for almost fifteen years. And while he was by no means wealthy, his practice supported a growing family and allowed him to volunteer for ACLU cases. Irons was particularly critical of Collins's "shotgun approach," which Ernest Besig described as "looking for every possible argument" and "dragging in most everything from soup to nuts." In an interview dating from the 1980s, Besig said, "Wayne was a little fox terrier with a machine-gun approach, which is not my way of doing business."

But during the 1940s, Besig stuck with Collins, refusing many opportunities to replace him during the two and a half years that the *Korematsu* case made its way through the federal court system. Roger Daniels, a distinguished historian of the Nikkei experience in the United States, agreed with Irons that a Collins legal brief "lacked the learned constitutional sophistication that scholars properly admire and practice." But Daniels believed that Collins "made the necessary legal points" and unlike other lawyers on the case, always concentrated on the most important issue: "securing the 'Blessings of Liberty' to tens of thousands of American citizens." For Wayne Collins, *Korematsu v. United States* was not just a legal case; it was also a moral crusade.

Fred Korematsu was one of just a handful of Japanese Americans who disobeyed the government orders and decrees. Some did so as a matter of principle. In Seattle, Gordon Hirabayashi, a

University of Washington graduate who was a Quaker and a conscientious objector, purposefully violated the curfew imposed on West Coast Nikkei as an act of civil disobedience. He also violated the subsequent assembly and removal orders. Similarly, Portland attorney Minoru Yasui sought to establish a test case by disobeying both the curfew and the order to assemble for evacuation. In Sacramento, Mitsuye Endo was one of sixty-three California state employees who challenged their dismissal from their jobs for the sole reason of Japanese ancestry. After their forced removal from Sacramento made the employment case moot, Endo agreed to serve as plaintiff in a legal challenge to the incarceration itself. The government offered her the chance to leave the camp at Topaz, Utah, but she refused so that her case would remain active.

By contrast, twenty-three-year-old Fred Korematsu initially acted primarily out of personal motives rather than political or moral principle. While he was certainly aware of the legal issues involved in his action, Korematsu just wanted to continue his normal life, exercising what the Declaration of Independence called his inalienable right to "life, liberty, and the pursuit of happiness." The son of Japanese immigrants, Korematsu grew up in Oakland, attending public school and working in his parents' San Leandro nursery. He became a shipyard welder but was fired because of his Japanese ancestry. He twice tried to join the army but was rejected because of an old injury and his ethnicity. Korematsu and his Italian American girlfriend, Ida Boitano, planned to marry, in spite of widespread public disapproval of such interracial relationships and the opposition of both sets of parents. Since California law prohibited interracial unions, the couple hoped to travel to Arizona. When his family reported for evacuation, Korematsu remained in

Oakland, claiming to be of Spanish and Hawaiian descent. He forged a draft card with the name Clyde Sarah and tried, with very little success, to change his appearance through plastic surgery. On May 31, 1942, San Leandro police arrested Korematsu and turned him over to federal authorities, who charged him with violating Public Law 503.

Looking for a case that could serve as a challenge to Executive Order 9066, Ernest Besig visited Korematsu shortly after his arrest. The two men hit it off, eventually establishing a personal friendship. Korematsu agreed to be represented by the Northern California ACLU branch (as well as agreeing to pay the two-dollar branch membership fee). Initially, Clarence Rust, a San Francisco lawyer and member of the branch board, served as Korematsu's attorney. But Besig asked Collins to take charge of the case. After Korematsu signed an attorney-client agreement, Collins began work on what was to become *Korematsu v. United States*. Though he didn't realize it at the time, Wayne Collins was embarking on a quarter-century-long legal battle on behalf of Nikkei rights and liberties.

Besig introduced Collins to Korematsu at a meeting at the Tanforan Assembly Center, actually a horseracing track in San Bruno. Fred was held there along with most other Bay Area Nikkei until the long-term camps were ready for occupancy. Korematsu considered Collins "a very intelligent man…a good man." According to legal scholar Lorraine Bannai, Collins was "the kind of person who would stick with a job until it was done. That tenaciousness was evident throughout Collins's representation of Fred." The two men seem to have had a typical attorney-client relationship that never developed into the kind of personal friendship that existed between Korematsu and Besig. It was Besig who had to deliver Ida

Boitano's message ending the engagement. However, Ida continued to defend her former fiancé in FBI interviews, insisting he was a loyal American citizen.

On June 20, 1942, Collins and Rust submitted a written brief, asking for a dismissal of charges against Fred Korematsu. The brief illustrated Collins's "shotgun approach," arguing the case on a variety of grounds, some of which Peter Irons, in his 1983 book, claimed "bordered on the frivolous." But even Irons admitted the core arguments went to the heart of the issues of removal and incarceration. Collins pointed out that since the Civil War, the Supreme Court had held that in time of war, civilians' constitutional rights must be protected, except "in a theater of war under martial law." Since there was no combat on the West Coast, and the president hadn't declared martial law, Collins argued that Executive Order 9066 was an unconstitutional extension of executive power. And since implementation of the order only applied to people of Japanese descent, it was racially motivated and violated the principle of equal protection of the law. If the executive order was unconstitutional, the military decrees that followed were an illegal "usurpation of legislative powers" and established a "military dictatorship" over the Nikkei. And Public Law 503, which enforced these improper orders and decrees, was itself an illegal extension of legislative power. Therefore, Collins claimed that the government had violated Fred Korematsu's Fifth Amendment rights by depriving him of life, liberty, and property without due process of law.

While Collins was preparing his brief, the national ACLU board was trying to arrive at a position on Executive Order 9066. Some board members agreed with Collins's opposition to the executive order, but a majority did not. Although the ACLU had its origins in the antiwar movement of World War I and opposition to the Red Scare that followed, historian Judy Kutulas observes that the organization had "repositioned itself as a mainstream liberal institution that could cooperate with a liberal government" (like the Roosevelt administration). Board members didn't want to be perceived as hurting the war effort or criticizing a popular president. Many on the board and staff had close ties with the administration, which they believed enhanced the ACLU's power and influence. After long debate, on June 22, 1942, the board voted by a two-to-one margin not to oppose Executive Order 9066. National Executive Director Roger Baldwin informed Besig of the decision and ordered the Northern California branch to withdraw from the *Korematsu* case. Baldwin pointed out that the branch could still challenge the improper implementation of the executive order, but not the order itself.

On July 2, Ernest Besig replied "we feel compelled to proceed as before." The Northern California branch had taken on *Korematsu* in good faith and was committed to pursue the case to its conclusion. Wayne Collins had already filed his brief and refused to withdraw it. On July 6, ACLU General Counsel Clifford Foster warned Besig not to argue "whether the government may constitutionally evacuate American citizens from any zone." On July 8, Foster said that if the branch "proceeded contrary to the policy of the national office," it would be "a violation of the bylaws." On July 9, Besig replied that the branch "cannot in good conscience" obey the national orders. Eventually, Besig simply stopped answering national office mail for two months. Meanwhile, Wayne Collins prepared for the court hearing on his dismissal motion, knowing he had the full support of the Northern California branch and its executive director.

The hearing took place on August 31, 1942, in the San Francisco federal courtroom of District Judge Martin I. Welch. A loyal Democrat, Welch was appointed to the bench by Franklin D. Roosevelt in 1939. He was a member of the notoriously anti-Asian Native Sons of the Golden West. According to Irons, Welch had a reputation as an "impetuous and lazy judge" who had political ambitions. He turned down the dismissal motion in a twenty-eight-word statement that did not mention any of the issues raised in Collins's long brief. Welch set the trial date for September 8, giving the lawyers just eight days to prepare.

Because Welch would be on vacation that week, the case was assigned to Judge Adolphus Frederic St. Sure. Unlike Welch, the seventy-three-year-old St. Sure was a powerful figure on the bench. According to a history of the Ninth Circuit Court, St. Sure was "respected, feared and seldom challenged." Appointed by President Calvin Coolidge in 1925, St. Sure had a somewhat progressive reputation. Whatever he may have thought of St. Sure, Collins was probably glad to be rid of Judge Welch.

Since Welch had dismissed Collins's constitutional arguments, the only issue in the trial was whether Fred Korematsu had violated Public Law 503 by refusing to report for the assembly and removal process. In fact, Korematsu readily admitted he had done just that. Other than establishing a record for an appeal, Collins's major job was trying to win a light sentence for his client. Given the state of wartime public opinion, Collins opted for a nonjury trial, putting his faith in Judge St. Sure's fairness. After the testimony of an FBI agent for the prosecution, Collins put Korematsu on the stand to tell his own story. It turned out to be an inspired move. Prosecutor Alfonso Zirpoli had called the defendant "a son of Nippon" perhaps trying to convey the image of a dangerous Japanese zealot. The soft-spoken, respectful witness was anything but that. Korematsu testified that he had tried to join the American armed forces. He had never been to Japan or claimed Japanese citizenship. His Japanese language skills were so poor that he needed one of his brothers to interpret when he talked to his mother. Korematsu even brought a bit of comic relief to the proceedings by telling the story of his plastic surgery fiasco. He guessed he didn't get much for the hundred dollars he paid for the procedure, because "when I went to the Tanforan Assembly Center, everyone knew me and my folks didn't know the difference."

The trial strategy worked. While St. Sure found the defendant guilty, the sentence was five years parole with no jail time. Collins said he would file an appeal and asked for his client to be released on bail. St. Sure agreed, first setting bail at $2,500 and then $5,000. After Besig posted bond, Korematsu was apparently free to leave. But a military police officer intervened, saying he had orders to keep the defendant in custody. The MP even pulled a gun from his holster, engaging in what Irons called "an armed revolt of the military against duly constituted judicial authority." Judge St. Sure finally allowed Korematsu to be returned to Tanforan.

Eventually, Korematsu and most other Bay Area Nikkei were removed to the Topaz camp in Utah. In 1943, camp authorities allowed Korematsu to move to Salt Lake City where he again worked as a welder. In 1944, he was allowed to relocate to Detroit, where he eventually married and started a family. Korematsu did not return to California until 1949, so he was unable to participate directly in Collins's judicial appeals. However, Besig kept Fred informed of developments and made sure he kept paying his Northern California branch dues.

After Korematsu's conviction, the national ACLU wanted the Northern California branch to disassociate itself from any appeal that Collins might file. Roger Baldwin considered Collins an irresponsible "lone wolf." Moreover, Baldwin regarded Fred Korematsu, with his white girlfriend, forged draft card, and attempted plastic surgery, as a deeply flawed defendant, who reflected badly on the ACLU's public image. Since Besig again refused to back down, Baldwin tried going over his head, communicating directly with Northern California board president Edward Parsons, an Episcopal bishop. Baldwin proposed that the branch withdraw from the case and let Collins proceed as Korematsu's private lawyer. But Bishop Parsons expressed support for the case, as well as for Besig and Collins. After weeks of fruitless back and forth between New York and San Francisco, Besig told Baldwin, "Please don't waste my time on the Korematsu controversy. I refuse to have any more to do with it."

Collins filed his appeal brief in the name of the rebellious Northern California branch, with no reference to the national ACLU. In it, Collins repeated most of his original arguments and included some of his characteristic rhetorical flourishes. He did make a special effort to defend the loyalty of West Coast Nisei. Although some had dual American and Japanese citizenship, Collins argued that just as the fact that American Catholics may have citizenship in the Vatican does not mean that "Catholics are subversive," Nisei dual citizenship didn't mean that Japanese Americans were disloyal.

The hearing on the appeal took place before the Ninth Circuit Court of Appeals in San Francisco on February 19, 1943. The court considered Korematsu's case along with those of Gordon

Hirabayashi and Minoru Yasui. Like Korematsu, both men had been convicted of violations of Public Law 503. The appellate court upheld all three convictions, making the cases eligible for Supreme Court consideration. But the high court chose to hear only the Hirabayashi and Yasui appeals. They had been convicted of violating General DeWitt's curfew, as well as the assembly and removal requirements. The justices decided to limit their initial review to the narrow issue of the curfew. Since Fred Korematsu had not been arrested for a curfew violation, the high court did not consider his case. However, Collins submitted an amicus, or friend of the court, brief for the Northern California branch on behalf of Gordon Hirabayashi.

On June 1, 1943, the Supreme Court unanimously upheld the Hirabayashi and Yasui convictions, establishing the constitutionality of Executive Order 9066 at least in the matter of the curfew. Even though the president had not declared martial law, the court found that there was a valid national security basis for the curfew. Roger Baldwin assumed this would be the court's final word on the executive order. But Wayne Collins filed a petition, asking the high court to review *Korematsu*. While the justices were considering the petition, Baldwin again told Besig the Northern California branch "should of course be separate from Mr. Collins." Besig replied, "Mr. Collins is attorney of record for Korematsu by reason of being counsel for the Northern California branch." The differences between New York and San Francisco were never fully resolved. They created a personal breach between Baldwin and Besig that lasted for the rest of their lives. In the 1980s, Besig recalled that Baldwin "was more of a government representative than an ACLU representative for a while." Baldwin eventually apologized, but according to Besig, "he didn't have the guts to stand up at the time."

On March 27, 1944, the Supreme Court granted Collins's petition, the justices agreeing to review *Korematsu*. Furthermore, the court would combine its consideration of the *Korematsu* case with a review of Mitsuye Endo's challenge of her ongoing incarceration. The Supreme Court was finally going to rule on the heart of the president's policy under Executive Order 9066: the forced assembly, removal, and incarceration of the West Coast Nikkei. Fred Korematsu, represented by Wayne Collins, would get his day in the nation's highest court. "Nice going," Fred wrote Besig.

The debates within the ACLU were well known, at least to insiders, during the 1940s. But it took the research of Peter Irons and Aiko Herzig-Yoshinaga in the 1980s to expose the equally contentious divisions within the Department of Justice over the conduct of the *Korematsu* case. A key figure in the conflict was Edward Ennis, director of the department's Alien Enemy Control Unit. A graduate of Columbia University law school, Ennis was a New Deal liberal with a concern for civil rights and civil liberties. Like many Justice Department lawyers, including Attorney General Francis Biddle, Ennis had initially opposed what was to become Executive Order 9066. But the Justice Department critics more than met their match in War Department supporters of the forced removal policy. Assistant Secretary of War John J. McCloy said that when it came to "a question of safety of the country," the Constitution "is just a scrap of paper to me." After Roosevelt issued the executive order, Ennis loyally supported it, even defending the removal policy before the Ninth Circuit Court of Appeals in 1942.

In 1944 the Justice Department assigned Ennis to prepare the legal brief that Solicitor General Charles Fahy would present to the Supreme Court in the *Korematsu* case. To counter Collins's claim of racial bias, Ennis was prepared to argue that the executive order and the subsequent implementation measures were motivated by valid military security concerns. To make that case, Ennis had to depend on General DeWitt's *Final Report: Japanese Evacuation from the West Coast, 1942,* which dealt with the military situation in the period immediately following the attack on Pearl Harbor. But in researching the matter, Ennis learned for the first time that the War Department had been forced to remove racist language from the report's original draft. Even more disturbing, some of DeWitt's most important assertions were contradicted by other government agencies. Reports of the Office of Naval Intelligence and the FBI denied DeWitt's claim of the widespread disloyalty of West Coast Nikkei. The Federal Communications Commission and the FBI found no evidence of the communications that DeWitt said existed between the Nikkei and Japanese ships in the Pacific.

Ennis and his colleague John Burling believed they had an ethical and legal obligation to report this new evidence to the court. Solicitor General Fahy vehemently disagreed. He realized the material could substantially strengthen Collins's arguments. Fahy prohibited Ennis and Burling from disclosing the information. Burling tried to use a footnote in the brief to at least indirectly present the evidence, but the note was discovered and rewritten. Faced with a conflict between moral duty and bureaucratic hierarchy, Ennis took an extraordinary step that may have violated fundamental legal ethics. He confidentially discussed the case with Roger Baldwin and other national ACLU staff members. Ennis urged the union to intervene in *Korematsu,* in effect asking the organization to oppose his own side in a case before the Supreme Court.

In the end, the national ACLU did intervene, but not directly in support of Collins's position on *Korematsu*. Instead, Baldwin and his colleagues decided to concentrate on the *Endo* case, which challenged the ongoing incarceration, or what the government called detention, of people of Japanese descent. The ACLU New York office argued that Executive Order 9066 covered the initial assembly and removal of people, not the subsequent incarceration. This allowed the national ACLU to advocate on behalf of thousands of incarcerated Nikkei, including Mitsuye Endo and Fred Korematsu, without directly supporting Wayne Collins's challenge to President Roosevelt's executive order. The national ACLU could also criticize General DeWitt's racist implementation of the executive order without specifically criticizing the president's action itself. In effect, the ACLU argued that, if done properly, forced assembly and removal might be legal, but long-term detention was not.

Roger Baldwin chose Charles Horsky to represent the national ACLU before the Supreme Court. A graduate of Harvard Law School, Horsky was a skillful, experienced attorney with good political and legal connections. He was a partner in a prestigious Washington, D.C., law firm and had previously worked for the US Solicitor General's Office. In Washington he was known as "a liberal member of a conservative law firm." For Roger Baldwin, then, Charles Horsky was everything that Wayne Collins was not: a well-regarded member of the nation's legal establishment. Baldwin made one last attempt to persuade the Northern California branch to drop Collins. He offered a united ACLU legal effort led by Horsky, but Besig and the branch board once again stuck with Collins. Baldwin also tried to persuade James Purcell, the San

Francisco lawyer who had been representing Mitsuye Endo for more than two years, to turn his case over to Horsky. Not surprisingly, Purcell flatly refused.

Charles Horsky met several times with Edward Ennis to plot ACLU legal strategy, meetings Horsky later admitted went beyond the bounds of professional propriety. Horsky's amicus brief emphasized the distinction between evacuation and detention, arguing the latter was the most important issue. Baldwin wanted Horsky to directly address the court, and asked Besig if Collins was open to sharing his time before the justices with the national ACLU attorney. Besig answered that neither he nor Collins had any objection to Horsky submitting a brief, but pointed out that Collins felt "very strongly that the National Office has been a hindrance not a help." That observation was, if anything, a vast understatement, given Collins's anger at the actions and attitudes of the New York staff.

Besig, however, admitted that Horsky was known to be "a good fellow." Baldwin sweetened his request with funds to pay some of the legal expenses incurred by the branch in the *Korematsu* case, though emphasizing that the money could not be used "for lawyer's fees which the contributor does not wish to pay." Collins was working pro bono, paying many of the expenses, including two trips to Washington, DC, out of his own pocket. Even though Baldwin specifically prohibited paying Collins's legal fees, funds to defray some of the expenses were welcome. In the end, Collins reluctantly agreed to share his time before the court with Horsky.

On October 11, 1944, Wayne Collins made his first and only appearance at the Supreme Court. A night-school graduate, he was sharing time with an elite attorney with a Harvard diploma. It must have been a daunting but exalting experience for the kid who grew up in an institution for poor and troubled boys. The two lawyers had agreed that Collins would lead off, attacking Executive Order 9066 and General DeWitt's exclusion orders head on. Horsky would follow, concentrating on the detention issue. In a slight softening of the national ACLU position, Horsky admitted that forced removal led to detention, thus linking the executive order and the incarceration.

In their briefs submitted to the court, both Collins and Horsky had vigorously attacked the reputation of General DeWitt. Peter Irons has said Collins's brief, which charged DeWitt with harboring a "messianic delusion," was "short on analysis and long on vituperation." Although he did not know the information that Ennis had discovered, Collins knew enough to charge the general with bigotry and argue that racism was the real motive for the forced removal. Collins quoted DeWitt's explanation as to why the military did not distinguish between Japanese citizens and American citizens of Japanese descent: "A Jap's a Jap." In his oral argument, Collins continued to insist that since there was no valid military purpose for the removal, the only explanation was racism. According to Irons, "Collins refused to budge," in spite of great skepticism on the part of some of the justices. An exasperated Justice Felix Frankfurter summed up Collins's position as, "there is no rational basis for the exclusion order."

On the other hand, Solicitor General Charles Fahy strongly affirmed that the policy was based on rational grounds of national security. He said that "no person in any responsible position has ever taken a contrary position," a statement clearly contradicted by Edward Ennis's evidence. Peter Irons concludes that Fahy lied to the court and thus "betrayed the people's trust" and "undermined the court's integrity." In 1983, forty years after the fact, US District Judge Marilyn Hall Patel overturned Fred Korematsu's conviction on grounds of Fahy's prosecutorial misconduct. In 2011, sixty-five years after the fact, Acting Solicitor General Neal Katyal admitted that his predecessor had failed to disclose important evidence and relied on racist arguments in the *Korematsu* case. Katyal said Fahy had discredited the office of Solicitor General.

In contrast to Collins, Charles Horsky and James Purcell had a relatively easy time arguing the issue of detention before the court. In his brief on the *Endo* case, Edward Ennis had admitted that neither Executive Order 9066 nor Public Law 503 specifically mentioned long-term incarceration. Peter Irons writes that the government had in effect surrendered on the issues raised by *Endo*. Therefore, it was no surprise that when the court announced its decisions on December 18, 1944, the justices unanimously found in favor of Mitsuye Endo and ordered her release from incarceration. Justice William Douglas's opinion found that the executive order did not apply to detention of loyal citizens once they had left the excluded zone. However, by a 6-3 majority, the court upheld Fred Korematsu's conviction and thus the constitutionality of Executive Order 9066 and its various implementation decrees. The court had accepted the national ACLU's original distinction between assembly and removal on the one hand, and incarceration on the other. The former was legal; the latter was not.

Justice Hugo Black's majority opinion in *Korematsu* took Collins's charges of racism seriously. Black wrote that, "all legal restrictions which curtail the civil rights of a single racial group are immediately suspect." Historian Greg Robinson believes Black was establishing the court's concept of "strict scrutiny" regarding issues of race that played a major role in the decision in *Brown v. Board of Education* a decade later. But in the *Korematsu* decision, Black went on to observe, "That is not to say that all such restrictions are unconstitutional." In *Korematsu*, Black argued there were valid security concerns that justified the president's order and the subsequent implementation measures. Justice Frankfurter's supporting opinion buttressed Black's argument that the court cannot second-guess the military on security matters, especially in time of war. Fred Korematsu, then, was convicted not because of his race, but because he violated a legal government policy.

Collins's arguments had greater influence with the three dissenting justices. Justice Frank Murphy said that absent a declaration of martial law, the exclusion "falls into the ugly abyss of racism." He argued that deferring to the judgment of the military cannot excuse "obvious racial discrimination." Justice Robert Jackson wrote that the court could not accept a "military expedient that has no place in law under the Constitution." He pointed out that an Italian American or German American on parole for a crime of treason could live on the West Coast, but a loyal citizen of Japanese descent could not. And Justice Owen Roberts asserted the facts of the case show "a clear violation of constitutional rights."

The decisions in *Korematsu* and *Endo* have never been reversed and so technically still stand as legal precedent. But as a practical matter, both decisions were moot on December 18, 1944. One day earlier, on December 17, the Roosevelt administration announced it was ending the policies of removal and incarceration. Beginning January 1, 1945, people of Japanese descent were welcome to return to their homes on the West Coast. The government estimated that all ten camps would be closed within a year. (All but Tule Lake made that deadline.) The fact that the announcement occurred just one day before the Supreme Court released its decisions may have been a coincidence. But it's more likely that sources within the court tipped off the administration and allowed it to act before the court decisions were released to the public. In a sense, then, Wayne Collins's determination to fight the *Korematsu* case all the way to the Supreme Court may have hastened the end of the removal and incarceration policy, freeing the West Coast Nikkei eight months before the end of the war itself.

In Detroit, Fred Korematsu said, "When I found out that I lost my decision, I thought I had lost my country." But he still took the time to write to Besig and thank him and the Northern California branch for their efforts on his behalf. And, he added, "Will you please give my thanks to and regards to Mr. Collins." Wayne Collins had lost a major battle, but he was soon to discover that he was not able to drop out of the legal war. His defense of the rights and liberties of people of Japanese descent in the United States was just beginning.

CHAPTER 4

TULE LAKE

Wayne Collins did not have to wait long for a scholarly response to the Supreme Court's decision in the *Korematsu* case. In June 1945, just six months after the decision, Yale Law professor Eugene Rostow published an article in the *Yale Law Journal* entitled "The Japanese American Cases—a Disaster." Rostow, who twenty years later would serve in President Lyndon Johnson's administration, said that, "One hundred thousand persons were sent to concentration camps on a record which wouldn't support a conviction for stealing a dog." Although Rostow did not mention any of the lawyers by name, he readily agreed with Collins's evaluation of General DeWitt's motives: "The general's motivation was ignorant race prejudice, not facts." Rostow also agreed with Justice Robert Jackson's observation in his dissenting opinion that the precedent established by *Korematsu* "lies like a loaded weapon ready for the hand of any authority that can bring forth a claim of urgent need."

As gratified as he must have felt reading Rostow's article, Collins was probably relieved to be finished with the *Korematsu* case. He was able to return to his regular law practice and concentrate on normal paying clients. He was also able to spend more time with his family. His daughter Margaret was three years old, and Thelma was pregnant with their second child, Wayne Merrill, who was born in April. Yet Collins's respite from the Nikkei cases lasted a little more than half a year. By the summer of 1945, events at the Tule Lake Segregation Center swept him into legal battles that were to last more than two decades and involve the constitutional rights of more than five thousand individuals.

Tule Lake was one of the ten long-term camps established to house the incarcerated Nikkei. Located in sparsely populated Modoc County in the high desert of northeastern California, the camp was near the bed of a shallow lake that had been partially drained in the 1920s to create land for irrigated agriculture. In the 1930s, the Roosevelt administration had established a Civilian Conservation Corps camp in the area. In the spring of 1942, the government began construction of the Nikkei camp. Rows of drab barrack-like buildings were built as living quarters. Barbed wire surrounded the camp, and soldiers patrolled the perimeter. By 1943, twelve thousand people were living at Tule Lake, making it the largest community in the region. Most of the people incarcerated in the camp were relocated from California's Sacramento Valley, but there were also residents from Oregon and Washington. Mitsuye Endo of the *Endo* case and, as we have seen, Hiroshi Kashiwagi were among those imprisoned at Tule Lake.

While the army carried out the initial evacuation and assembly and provided security, the president created a civilian agency, the War Relocation Authority, to run the camps. The WRA was initially part of the War Department and later moved to the Department of the Interior. WRA administrators and staff exercised ultimate authority, but Nikkei labor was essential to the operation of the camp. The incarcerated residents worked in offices, clinics, schools, kitchens, agricultural fields, et cetera. Basic wage for such labor was sixteen dollars per month, almost what a war worker in a San Francisco Bay Area shipyard could make in a day with overtime added to the regular pay. Wayne Collins criticized WRA bureaucrats for using camp inmates as domestic servants at the sixteen-dollar-per-month rate.

According to official WRA terminology, camps like Tule Lake were "relocation units," but critics like Wayne Collins called them concentration camps. In the summer of 1943, the WRA rechristened Tule Lake as a "segregation center" so that it could house people from the other nine camps who were designated as "disloyals" and "troublemakers." Workers installed additional barbed wire and built new watchtowers. The army increased the number of soldiers and even stationed six old tanks at the facility. Now, more than ever, Tule Lake took on the character of a concentration camp.

Dillon S. Myer, director of the War Relocation Authority, had made the decision to transform Tule Lake into a restrictive "segregation center." When the WRA was established in 1942, President Roosevelt appointed Milton Eisenhower, a Department of Agriculture administrator and brother of General Dwight Eisenhower, as director of the new agency. After just ninety days on the job, Milton Eisenhower accepted another government position and recommended Dillon Myer, his Department of Agriculture colleague, as his successor. Eisenhower advised Myer to accept the job only if he could do it "and sleep at night." Myer later said, "I was sure I could sleep, and so I accepted the position." But after a few months, he, like Eisenhower before him, came to believe that the removal and incarceration was unnecessary, unjust, and probably unconstitutional. A New Deal liberal, Myer believed that America's racial problems would be solved by assimilation, bringing minority group members into the white middle class mainstream. The incarceration program was having exactly the opposite effect. Myer's aim was "getting these people out of the relocation centers and reestablished in normal communities."

Unable to end the incarceration outright, Myer sought to build on a program that originally allowed West Coast Nisei college students to transfer to educational institutions outside of the restricted zone rather than be imprisoned in camps. Now Myer proposed that the government permit other loyal Nikkei to leave the camps and settle in communities in the Midwest or on the East Coast. Although initially opposed by General DeWitt and politicians like California governor Earl Warren, the "furlough" program gradually gained traction. Myer hoped that by concentrating alleged "disloyals" and "troublemakers" at Tule Lake, he could increase the number of furloughs of "loyal" residents from the other nine camps. By the end of 1944, about one quarter of the formerly incarcerated Nikkei were living outside of the camps. Among that group was Fred Korematsu, who, as we have seen, settled first in Salt Lake City and then in Detroit.

Myer had the strong backing of the Fair Play Committee, a Berkeley-based group of citizens supporting the Nikkei. Though the committee had only about six hundred members, they included such prominent figures as University of California president Robert Gordon Sproul and documentary photographer Dorothea Lange. The committee's executive secretary, Ruth Kingman, was a well-known Bay Area liberal and a member of the Northern California branch of the American Civil Liberties Union who knew both Ernest Besig and Wayne Collins. On behalf of the Fair Play Committee, Kingman made two lobbying trips to Washington, DC, and won a sympathetic hearing from Attorney General Francis Biddle and Secretary of the Interior Harold Ickes. Even President Roosevelt's daughter, Anna, became sympathetic to the committee's cause.

But the Fair Play Committee's most important Washington ally was Dillon Myer. Kingman and other committee leaders shared Myer's objections to the incarceration and agreed with his assimilationist views on racial matters. They strongly supported his furlough program, as well as his efforts to establish a very limited form of self-government in the camps. From the Fair Play Committee's perspective, concentrating so-called disloyals and troublemakers at Tule Lake would reassure the public about the loyalty of the great majority of the Nikkei in the other nine camps and help build support for an eventual end of incarceration. A remarkable, if bizarre, alliance had developed between the best-known group that opposed Executive Order 9066 and the man responsible for administering it.

Myer also had the backing of the Japanese American Citizens League, whose members were primarily college-educated young Nisei committed to assimilating into the mainstream of American life. The JACL initially questioned the need for the removal and incarceration, but once the president made his decision, the organization urged Nikkei to obey the executive order as loyal American citizens and legal residents. The JACL initially opposed the *Korematsu* case, disassociating the organization from both Wayne Collins and his working-class client. However, after the national ACLU reluctantly entered the case, the JACL hired A. L. Wirin, a prominent Southern California civil rights lawyer, to submit an amicus brief to the Supreme Court on behalf of the Japanese American Citizens League.

In the camps, JACL members often worked closely with WRA staff, hoping to create camp administrations that were humane, orderly, and efficient. The organization enthusiastically supported Myer's furlough program, and like him urged the Department of War to allow Nisei to serve in the armed forces. In 1943, the government permitted camp residents to volunteer for the army, and in 1944, young Nisei men became eligible for the draft. Many JACL members served with distinction in the all-Nisei 442nd Regimental Combat Team.

But by no means all Nikkei accepted JACL leadership and values. A small minority, including some Kibei (Nisei who as children were sent to Japan for their education), openly supported Japan in the war. Some Issei resented the fact that the JACL was no longer deferring to the traditional Japanese-born leadership of the Nikkei community. And many Nisei opposed cooperation and collaboration with a US government that was denying their basic constitutional rights and liberties. In late 1942 and early 1943, there were sometimes violent strikes and protests in several camps, including Tule Lake. Often the targets were WRA staff and their JACL allies. For the JACL leaders, then, their support for Dillon Myer's establishment of a segregation center at Tule Lake might have been a matter of personal security as well as ideology. If the "troublemakers" most likely to lead protests were at Tule Lake, JACL members at the other nine camps might no longer be targeted.

In 1943, a WRA security questionnaire that camp inhabitants were required to answer included two questions designed to test the loyalty of the Nikkei. Question 27 asked if the person surveyed would serve in the American armed forces, while question 28 inquired if the respondent would forswear all allegiance to Japan and the Japanese emperor. The questions caused debate, consternation, and social upheaval among much of the camp population. Even Dillon Myer admitted his agency had erred in including these issues in the questionnaire. In the end, the great majority of camp residents, including Fred Korematsu, answered "yes" to both questions. But there were still several thousand people who answered "no, no" or left the questions blank. The WRA designated most of these individuals as disloyal and relocated them to the newly designated Tule Lake Segregation Center.

During the summer and early fall of 1943, Tule Lake experienced seismic demographic and social changes. The twelve thousand existing inmates could choose either to move to another camp or stay in the reorganized segregation center. About half the old inmates, including Mitsuye Endo, moved, while the rest, including Hiroshi Kashiwagi, chose to remain at Tule Lake. Twelve thousand newcomers moved in, including people designated as "disloyals" and "troublemakers," along with their families. With more than eighteen thousand inmates, Tule Lake became the largest of the ten WRA centers. Since the planned capacity was fifteen thousand, the facility was seriously overcrowded. There were tensions between old and new residents, pro-Japanese demonstrators and loyal JACL members, and between activists who protested against camp authorities and those who hoped to avoid trouble by keeping a low profile.

On October 16, 1943, a truck filled with farm workers from the camp overturned, killing one person and injuring several others. Camp residents organized a farm workers' strike and elected a Daihyo Sha Kai, a community council, to negotiate with the administration. The council demanded administrative policy changes, as well as improvements in working conditions for farm laborers and other camp employees. Tule Lake director Raymond Best refused to negotiate, and brought in strikebreakers from other camps, paying them considerably more than the standard sixteen dollars per month. On November 1, Dillon Myer visited Tule Lake and was met by large protests. He held a tense, unproductive session with council representatives, while at least five thousand demonstrators gathered around the building where the meeting was held. Although the crowd remained peaceful, some WRA staff feared for their safety. The camp administration ordered additional barbed wire fences erected to protect the homes of the white staff.

On November 14, 1943, the army declared martial law, the military taking over the administration of Tule Lake. The facility quite literally became an armed camp. The army arrested about two hundred alleged ringleaders, including members of the elected Daihyo Sha Kai. The prisoners were placed in a hastily constructed stockade, and in some cases suffered brutal beatings at the hands of the military guards. Civilian WRA administrators took back control of the camp on January 15, 1944, and released some of the prisoners. But the stockade remained open with several people still in custody. Although there were no trials or other forms of due process, some prisoners stayed in the facility for as long as ten months. Inmates staged hunger strikes to protest their continued imprisonment and the harsh conditions inside the stockade. One stockade prisoner, Ernest Kozumatu, said, "no reason was ever given for my arrest." He was held "without trial and sentence." He reported that food and other living conditions improved somewhat after the WRA regained control from the army, but authorities censored the mail under both regimes.

In the spring of 1944, sympathetic WRA staff members informed Ernest Besig of the situation at Tule Lake. Besig decided to travel there to investigate conditions and interview plaintiffs for a possible lawsuit. But Dillon Myer, backed by ACLU Executive Director Roger Baldwin, refused to allow the visit. Besig wrote directly to Secretary of the Interior Harold Ickes and in late June finally received permission to make the trip. He arrived at Tule Lake on July 10 and was received with something less than open arms by the camp administration. Camp managers allowed him to interview Nikkei inmates only in the presence of WRA staff. As the tense visit proceeded, Dillon Myer asked Roger Baldwin if he would object to Besig being removed. When Baldwin raised no objection, camp staff banned Besig from Tule Lake. The WRA explained that he could return only if he was formally representing a camp resident in a legal case.

Besig's car was parked in the camp lot, and he discovered that during his stay, someone had poured salt in the gas tank. He demanded that the WRA reimburse him for damages. Dillon Myer expressed sympathy but said he couldn't believe a WRA employee would be responsible for such a dastardly act. The August 1944 issue of the *American Civil Liberties News*, the Northern California branch's official newsletter, summed up Besig's experience at the camp with the headline "Tyranny Begins at Tule Lake."

Once again, Ernest Besig turned to Wayne Collins. Although Collins was in the midst of preparing for his October Supreme Court appearance in the *Korematsu* case, Besig asked him to take on representation of the men in the Tule Lake stockade. Never one to avoid a legal battle in defense of constitutional liberties, Collins began discussions with R. B. Cozzens, head of the WRA regional office in San Francisco. Collins demanded the men be released from the stockade, since they had been imprisoned without due process and thus denied their basic Fifth Amendment rights. Cozzens replied that those in the stockade were "troublemakers" who had been "separated," not imprisoned. Such linguistic distinctions were lost on Wayne Collins, and the discussions became heated. Collins finally prepared a brief for a habeas corpus writ, asking a federal district judge to release the men from unlawful detention. He threatened to bring the case to federal court unless the WRA released the prisoners immediately.

Wayne Collins delivered his ultimatum at a meeting at the WRA office in San Francisco on August 22, 1944. In addition to Cozzens, the WRA chief counsel Philip Glick and Tule Lake camp director Raymond Best attended the session. During the meeting, they were joined by Dillon Myer, whom Collins described as looking tired and suffering from "lameness." The upheavals at Tule Lake had taken a heavy toll on Myer and his agency. The Hearst newspapers, among others, had called for Myer's dismissal, arguing that he had "coddled" the camp prisoners. California governor Earl Warren proposed abolishing the WRA and putting all camps under permanent military control. Now Myer was faced with a possible habeas corpus suit that would generate heavy publicity and possibly alienate liberal supporters in groups like the Fair Play Committee. In the end, Myer agreed to the demand. While Collins looked on, Raymond Best phoned Tule Lake and ordered all prisoners released and the stockade closed. A few days later, Collins traveled to Tule Lake and reported that almost "no vestige of the stockade is discernible." Wayne Collins had won his first victory on behalf of Nikkei rights.

While Collins was successfully representing the prisoners at Tule Lake, Ernest Besig had been playing his familiar role of holding off the ACLU national office. At one point, Besig had invited Roger Baldwin to come to Tule Lake and see conditions in the stockade for himself. Predictably, Baldwin declined the offer. On August 7, 1944, the ACLU general counsel Clifford Foster had ordered the Northern California branch to take no further action on the stockade matter until the national board met on August 21. Among other things, the New York office wanted to consult with Dillon Myer. The board canceled its August meeting, so Foster said the matter would be delayed until September. Besig must have been delighted to inform New York that the prisoners had been released from the stockade on August 24. Besig explained that the Northern California branch contemplated no further action on the matter; there was no longer any need for the national board to discuss the issue.

Collins's victory had an impact on camp morale. Virtually isolated from the outside world and shunned by the national ACLU, the JACL, and the Fair Play Committee, Tule Lake inmates recognized they nonetheless had effective allies in the Northern California branch of the ACLU in general, and Ernest Besig and Wayne Collins in particular. In July of 1945, almost a year after his first legal battle at Tule Lake, camp residents informed Collins that the WRA had reopened the stockade and imprisoned several young men. Once again, Collins made the long drive to Tule Lake, and once again he closed down the stockade.

But while in the camp, Collins was approached by a few Issei parents who said their grown Nisei children had renounced their American citizenship and were facing deportation to Japan. To his amazement, Collins learned that these were not isolated cases. More than five thousand people, about 70 percent of the adult Nisei population of the camp, had given up their rights and identity as US citizens. And now their former government was planning to send them on a one-way trip to Japan. Wayne Collins's respite from the Nikkei cases was over. He was going to have to figure out a way to help five thousand Japanese Americans win back their rights as citizens of the United States of America.

CHAPTER 5

RENUNCIANTS

Wayne Collins's reaction to the widespread renunciation of citizenship at Tule Lake was that "you can no more resign citizenship in time of war than you can resign from the human race." The Fourteenth Amendment to the Untied States Constitution provides that anyone born in the United States is an American citizen. Ratified in 1868, the amendment was part of the Congressional Reconstruction program following the Civil War. One of its purposes was to assure that the recently freed former slaves received all the rights and privileges of citizenship. But the concept of "birthright citizenship" also became a key component of American immigration policy. No matter what the legal status of their parents, the Constitution provided that all American-born second-generation immigrants were full-fledged US citizens. And Wayne Collins argued that citizens could not simply give up the rights granted to them by the Constitution.

Immigration opponents and restrictionists have often attempted to change or subvert the Fourteenth Amendment's definition of citizenship. In the pre–World War II period, the California Joint Immigration Committee, a vehemently anti-Japanese organization founded in 1921 by former *Sacramento Bee* publisher Valentine S. McClatchy, argued that the constitutional provisions applied only to children of European immigrants. In our own time, politicians like Donald Trump have advocated denying citizenship to children of undocumented immigrants whom he and many of his supporters call "anchor babies." During World War II, several members of Congress favored legislation that would strip Japanese Americans of their citizenship status (while maintaining citizenship rights for German Americans and Italian Americans). Department of Justice liberals, including Attorney General Francis Biddle and Director of the Alien Enemy Control Unit Edward Ennis, fought against these congressional proposals, arguing that only another constitutional amendment could change the clear language of the Fourteenth Amendment that provided for birthright citizenship without regard to race, nationality, or the legal status of immigrant parents.

But Biddle, Ennis, and many of their Justice Department colleagues believed that there was a need to deal with the citizenship status of the allegedly disloyal Nisei individuals at Tule Lake. If the government could not deprive them of their citizenship, how could it deport such people from the United States? The solution was Public Law 405, which for the first time allowed citizens residing in the United States to voluntarily renounce their American nationality. The law's supporters assumed that disloyal people would welcome the chance to end their status as citizens of a country to which they had no allegiance. Since the decision was voluntary, Justice Department lawyers argued it did not violate the Fourteenth Amendment. Persons wishing to take advantage of the law could petition the Attorney General, and the Justice Department was required to investigate each request to assure that it was truly voluntary. The legislation passed both houses of Congress and was signed into law by President Roosevelt on July 1, 1944. There was now a legal mechanism for the voluntary termination of American citizenship for residents of the United States.

Public Law 405 profoundly affected Tule Lake. The Justice Department ultimately approved virtually all the renunciation applications it received, including 5,461 from Tule Lake and just 128 applications from all the other nine camps combined. These statistics reflected the chaotic situation at Tule Lake in late 1943 and early 1944. In the aftermath of the imposition of martial law and the establishment of the stockade in 1944, the pro-Japan minority at Tule Lake became the most active segment of the camp's population. Pro-Japan militants organized two groups, the Hoshi-dan and the Hokoku-dan, to advocate on behalf of Japanese identity and patriotism. Out of a camp population of eighteen thousand, the groups eventually had about a thousand active members, mostly Issei and second-generation Kibei, who had spent part of their childhoods in Japan. The organizations held morning exercises and military calisthenics and paraded to martial bugle calls. They labeled their opponents "white Japanese" and "Inu" (dogs) and sometimes backed up those insults with beatings and other forms of physical intimidation. In spite of this, the camp administration allowed the organizations to operate for several months.

After the passage of Public Law 405, the pro-Japan militants called for Tule Lake residents to renounce their American citizenship. By the beginning of December 1944, about six hundred renunciations had occurred. As we have seen, on December 17, the government ended mandatory incarceration and announced that all camps would close within a year. Most Nikkei outside of Tule Lake welcomed the end of removal and incarceration. But in the troubled atmosphere of Tule Lake, many residents interpreted the change of policy as a plot to force the Nikkei into dangerous white communities filled with violent racists. Militants argued that renunciation would allow individuals to remain in the comparative safety of the camp until repatriation to Japan. A popular (and incorrect) rumor at Tule Lake had it that after the war the government would deport all Issei from the United States. Pro-Japan activists claimed that the only way that families could stay together was for Nisei to renounce their citizenship and accompany their Issei parents to Japan. Finally, many Nisei regarded renunciation as a gesture of protest against the government's violation of their basic rights and liberties.

The direct result of all these fears, assumptions, and resentments was an avalanche of renunciation at Tule Lake. By the end of December 1944, the government had received 1,200 renunciation applications from the camp. In January 1945, there were another 3,400. By March the total was over 5,400. Seventy percent of the eligible Nisei population at Tule Lake had renounced their American citizenship, and 97 percent of all Nisei petitions for renunciation had come from the Tule Lake camp.

Haruko Inouye was one of the Tule Lake renunciants. Twenty years old when she filed her petition, she said it was simply a "matter of family unity." Since her family believed that the Issei would be sent back to Japan, she renounced her citizenship so that she could accompany her parents. Akiko Fukuhara was also bound by family ties. The eighteen-year-old was ordered to give up her citizenship by her parents so that the family could stay together. Similarly, it was Hiroshi Kashiwagi's mother who asked him to renounce. Kashiwagi also felt threatened by pro-Japanese activists. He said "it was too dangerous to try to be different." Once he renounced, he believed he "was no longer in danger of separation, relocation, and physical harm." Minoru Kiyota was "not fool enough to join Hokoku Dan or Hoshi Dan," but he so feared the organizations' threats of physical violence that he broke out in hives. He said he renounced "to express my fury toward the government of the United States.…It was the last act of defiance available to human beings who found themselves in an intolerable situation."

The Justice Department assigned attorney John Burling to monitor the renunciation process at Tule Lake. In theory, government agents interviewed each applicant to assure that the request was voluntary and the result of an informed decision. In fact, Minoru Kiyota reported that the whole renunciation petition process took barely ten minutes. This may have been because the interviewers were overwhelmed. Burling and his boss Edward Ennis had expected a few hundred people to renounce. Instead thousands of Nisei turned in applications. Burling and Ennis were stunned by the volume of requests, but they ended up approving virtually all the Tule Lake petitions. Once citizenship was renounced, the government classified the person as an enemy alien. As Ennis explained to petitioner Takashi Furuya, "Since you are an alien and since you are a person of Japanese ancestry and a person who has shown loyalty to Japan by voluntarily renouncing his United States citizenship," Furuya was now "a national of Japan" and an "enemy alien." This in spite of the fact that Furuya had formally renounced his Japanese citizenship in 1935. Like most renunciants, he was now technically a man without a country.

In July 1945, President Harry Truman issued Presidential Proclamation 2655, providing that "all dangerous enemy aliens" were "subject to removal from the United States." The Justice Department assumed this applied to the renunciants. The possibility of deportation panicked many Nisei. Even Hokoku members claimed they had been "misled and misinformed" by the organization's leaders. The deportation order did not apply to most Issei parents, so Nisei children no longer needed to renounce to maintain family unity. Indeed, it was more likely that the renunciants themselves faced deportation than their parents.

Like Hiroshi Kashiwagi, many of the petitioners believed they had been a "victim of the government's manipulation," that the government had encouraged them to renounce so that they could be deported. Minoru Kiyota said that when he renounced, "I walked right into a trap set by the U.S. government." The deportation proclamation "was the culmination of decades of calculated discrimination against Japanese Americans." About a thousand Tule Lake renunciants accepted voluntary "repatriation" to Japan. But that left more than four thousand who wished to stay in the United States. By August 1945, a growing number of them wanted their American citizenship back.

Wayne Collins's presence at Tule Lake in the late summer of 1945 was an impetus to activism. He advised renunciants to write immediately to the new attorney general, Tom Clark, and the director of the Alien Enemy Control Unit, Edward Ennis, withdrawing their renunciation petition and requesting a full restoration of citizenship. Collins drafted a sample letter, which was mimeographed and widely distributed throughout the camp. The letter emphasized that when people had applied for renunciation, they were under the duress of incarceration, subject to threats of violence, and acting on the basis of false rumors and inaccurate information. The letter writer could include personal stories and experiences to document these conditions. Soon the Justice Department was receiving hundreds, and eventually thousands, of such letters from Tule Lake renunciants.

Surprisingly, camp director Raymond Best supported the effort. His hard-line opposition to the farm workers' strike had helped create a crisis that brought martial law to Tule Lake in 1944. Best had also been hostile to Ernest Besig's visit to the camp and had opposed Wayne Collins's successful efforts to close the camp stockade. But now Best and WRA Director Dillon Myer criticized the Department of Justice's hard-line stance on renunciation. Best allowed the renunciants to organize and hold mass meetings at the camp and even wrote letters of support for some of those attempting to recover their citizenship.

However, neither Raymond Best nor the WRA controlled the renunciants' future. Their fate was in the hands of the US Department of Justice. The new attorney general, Tom Clark, had been a Justice Department lawyer during the early 1940s and, unlike most of his colleagues, had strongly backed Executive Order 9066. He now took a hard, uncompromising stand regarding the renunciants. They had made their choice and now had to live with it. Edward Ennis, the Justice Department's director of the Alien Enemy Control Unit, had direct authority over the new "enemy aliens." We have seen that Ennis had previously opposed the executive order and tried to expose the racism and factual inaccuracies of General DeWitt's *Final Report*. But nonetheless Ennis agreed with Clark regarding the renunciants. Ennis's replies to the letters from Tule Lake rarely dealt with the circumstances or personal matters brought up by the petitioners. Instead, he simply stated that there was no legal procedure to withdraw a renunciation of citizenship. As he told Akiko Fukuhara: once she had renounced, she "ceased to be a United States national."

Collins had expected this response and told the renunciants that they probably would have to take legal action. They needed to find a lawyer and organize a committee to manage a complicated lawsuit involving hundreds if not thousands of plaintiffs. The person who did most to establish the human infrastructure for the lawsuit was Tetsujiro "Tex" Nakamura. Born in San Francisco in 1917, Nakamura graduated from the University of California in 1939 with a degree in political science. He wanted to go to law school but could not immediately afford it so became a staff member for a Sacramento Nisei law firm. Incarcerated at Tule Lake, he took a job as a camp legal aide, presumably at the sixteen-dollar-per-month wage. When Tule Lake became a segregation center, Nakamura stayed on. Although he did not renounce his own US citizenship, he gave legal assistance and advice to the renunciants.

In the summer and fall of 1945, Nakamura followed Collins's advice and began organizing what became the Tule Lake Defense Committee. It was made up of renunciants and some of their family members and friends. Governed by a five-member all-male executive committee, the organization was designed to be the manager of the lawsuit, serving as the intermediary between the plaintiffs and their attorney. During the group's thirteen-year history, Tex Nakamura usually served as the committee staff person and de facto executive secretary. Classified by the government as a "loyal citizen," he was able to leave Tule Lake in August of 1945 and contact several attorneys on behalf of the defense committee. But he found no one willing to take the case. He received little support from either the national ACLU or the JACL. The former, with its close ties to Edward Ennis, initially supported the government position on renunciation. And significant numbers of JACL members considered the renunciants little more than traitors. Nakamura did get a sympathetic hearing from Ernest Besig, who promised public and moral support from the Northern California branch of the American Civil Liberties Union. But he made it clear that the organization had no funds to spare.

Besig, of course, recommended that Nakamura hire Wayne Collins. Collins had already turned down an offer to represent the renunciants, but now he felt morally obligated to take the job. He set two conditions: at least several hundred people willing to serve as plaintiffs for a class action lawsuit and adequate funding for a serious and possibly protracted legal battle. In September 1945, his offer was accepted at a mass meeting of about a thousand people at Tule Lake. In October, he agreed to a contract with the Tule Lake Defense Committee's five-member leadership group: Harry Uchida, Yasuo Honda, Yoshiro Kaku, Fumio Masuoka, and George Tsuetaki. Collins didn't realize at the time that he had signed on to a case that was to last for most of the rest of his life.

Tex Nakamura and Wayne Collins worked together on the case for more than a decade. Initially, Nakamura operated out of Collins's San Francisco office. Later he moved to Los Angeles and established the defense committee's headquarters in that city's Little Tokyo, the most important Japanese American community on the West Coast. In a 2009 interview conducted when he was ninety-two years old, Nakamura still had vivid memories of his colleague: "He was Irish; he had a hot temper." Nakamura would often accompany Collins to Justice Department hearings where Collins would "confront government officials and let renunciants know they had rights." The two men didn't agree on politics; Nakamura was a Republican, while Collins was a nonpartisan rebel, if not radical. During one presidential campaign, Collins told Nakamura he was going to write in "Mahatma Gandhi," since none of the candidates on the ballot deserved his support. But Collins and Nakamura agreed on the issue of renunciant rights and shared a common contempt for the positions of the national ACLU and the JACL. Nakamura finally got his law degree in 1956 and started his own legal practice. He said he learned "quite a bit from Collins." "The work [Collins] did was tremendous…but I had no idea I would be stuck with it so long."

The defense committee had asked each plaintiff to contribute one hundred dollars to help defray legal expenses. In the 1950s, the amount was raised to three hundred dollars. By November 1945, the committee had recruited almost a thousand parties to the suit, six hundred of whom had made the initial hundred-dollar payment. Eventually, nearly all the 5,400 renunciants joined the case, including most of those who had voluntarily relocated to Japan. Nakamura estimated that over its thirteen years of operation, the committee collected between $700,000 and $800,000 ($7 to $8 million in today's dollars). Most of the money was deposited in two San Francisco bank accounts from which Collins could withdraw and spend funds, subject to loose oversight by the executive committee. At the committee's request, he sometimes took money from one of the accounts, sending the funds to Los Angeles to meet executive committee expenses. At its height, the case cost about fifty thousand dollars per year. Nakamura claimed that Collins operated on a pro bono basis, but, in fact, Collins used the defense committee accounts to meet legal expenses and, in at least some years, to pay for his own professional services. Unlike the *Korematsu* case, then, Wayne Collins received some compensation for his protracted defense of the renunciants.

On November 13, 1945, Collins filed two lawsuits on behalf of 987 Tule Lake plaintiffs. One was a habeas corpus action to prevent the involuntary deportation of renunciants and free them from incarceration. The other, which became the case of *Abo v. Clark*, demanded the full restoration of United States citizenship. (Tadayasu Abo was the first plaintiff on the alphabetical list, while Tom Clark as attorney general stood for the United States government.) Collins questioned the constitutionality of Public Law 405, but his main argument attacked the government claim that the plaintiffs had voluntarily chosen to renounce their citizenship. He argued that the choice had occurred in the context of an unnecessary and improper incarceration and a chaotic and dangerous camp environment. The government neither protected Tule Lake residents from the violent threats and coercion of pro-Japan activists nor provided accurate information to counter frightening rumors. Therefore, the plaintiffs acted under conditions of significant duress that made a truly voluntary decision impossible. This was particularly true for the approximately one thousand renunciants who were minors under twenty-one years of age.

Collins also attacked the government's plan to deport the renunciants as enemy aliens, pointing out that the United States was no longer at war. He criticized the inadequate "pseudo hearings" the Justice Department held on individual renunciations. Finally, he included plenty of the old fashioned moralistic rhetoric that was so characteristic of a Collins legal brief. He claimed that since 1942, the government had waged "a form of war" against Japanese Americans "simply because of the geographical origin of their forbearers." The government, he said, "endeavored to deaden the minds and destroy the spirits" of the Nisei, and at Tule Lake "it nearly succeeded." "The spirit of brute force hovers over the land and evil practices are tolerated, sanctioned, and justified." He claimed that what "the government has done to these citizens will be enshrined in one word and that word is 'shameful.'" Collins followed up the brief with a letter to Attorney General Clark, which summed up the arguments for the plaintiffs: The renunciations were "neither real, free, nor voluntary" but were "obtained through duress, menace, fraud, undue influence and mistake of fact and law."

Judge Adolphus St. Sure initially presided over *Abo v. Clark*, just as he had in the *Korematsu* case. At Collins's request, St. Sure granted an injunction temporarily stopping the deportations. Collins had to serve the injunction order on a ship at San Francisco's Fort Mason to prevent the imminent deportation of renunciants to Japan. The government won a delay in the case so that it could hold "mitigation hearings" to determine which renunciants were subject to immediate deportation. The hearings occurred at Tule Lake, as well as at the Justice Department immigrant internment camps in Santa Fe, New Mexico, and Fort Lincoln, North Dakota. The WRA had eventually cracked down on the activities of the Hoshi-dan and Hokoku-dan and moved several hundred members from Tule Lake to the Justice Department camps in New Mexico and North Dakota. As a result, Collins, Nakamura, and Theodore Tamba, a San Francisco attorney who often worked with Collins, traveled to Santa Fe and Fort Lincoln to consult with the former Tule Lake prisoners. Many of the latter signed on, producing additional plaintiffs for the case.

The mitigation hearings took place between January and April of 1946. They resulted in the government granting most renunciants "stays of deportation" and freeing them from incarceration in the three camps. This allowed Tule Lake, the last operating WRA facility, finally to close in March. The freed renunciants could now live more or less normal lives as temporary resident aliens, but they still faced the possibility of future deportation, depending on the outcome of *Abo v. Clark*.

While freeing most of the renunciants from incarceration, the Justice Department kept 449 individuals in custody. They were still considered "disloyals" and were scheduled for immediate deportation if Judge St. Sure lifted his injunction. The government imprisoned them at an immigration facility at Crystal City, Texas, though some were allowed to work in a food processing plant in Seabrook, New Jersey. Tex Nakamura traveled to Crystal City and after consulting with the prisoners, signed up additional plaintiffs. For Nakamura and Collins, government-defined "disloyalty" was not a crime. United States citizens had the right to exercise freedom of thought. As long as they obeyed the law, citizens should be able to live and work in this country without government interference. Thus, even former members of the Hoshi-dan and Hokoku-dan were allowed to join the lawsuit.

During the last half of 1946, there was little progress in the case of *Abo v. Clark*. Collins jousted over preliminary motions with government lawyers, including Thomas Cooley who had replaced Edward Ennis as director of the Justice Department's Alien Enemy Control Unit. Collins attempted to introduce into evidence a letter by Under Secretary of the Interior Abe Fortas, which said that terror and coercion were the cause of 80 percent of the renunciations. Judge

St. Sure eventually refused to allow the letter, ruling it was a personal communication rather than an official government document.

The government also introduced an affidavit by Rosalie Hankey, a University of California graduate student participating in a study at Tule Lake led by sociologist Dorothy Swaine Thomas. Hankey's testimony actually seemed to support Collins's arguments. She said that Tule Lake residents who opposed renunciation "stood in danger of physical violence." But the most important early development in the case occurred in February 1947, when Judge St. Sure was incapacitated by illness. As a result, Judge Lewis E. Goodman took over *Abo v. Clark*. In Judge Goodman, Wayne Collins was to discover a kindred spirit.

Appointed to the federal bench by President Roosevelt in 1942, Goodman was born in the rural Central Valley community of Lemoore and grew up in San Francisco. He graduated from the University of California and Hastings School of Law. Son of Jewish immigrant parents, he was an outspoken critic of racism. According to a history of the Ninth Circuit Court, Goodman had a reputation as "a practical man with liberal leanings." His first exposure to Tule Lake came in 1944 when he presided over the trial of twenty-six Tule Lake residents who had resisted the draft.

After incarcerated Nisei men became eligible for selective service in 1944, they were required to go through the process of draft registration. A few hundred individuals in several WRA camps refused to register, saying they would not cooperate with the draft until the government restored their civil liberties. Local federal attorneys charged the draft resisters with violation of the Selective Service Act, and federal judges routinely found them guilty. Each year a federal district judge from San Francisco was assigned to spend a week hearing cases in the California north coast town of Eureka. The trip was scheduled for the summer and was considered something of a lark, with the judge and his staff spending time in the redwoods, being wined and dined by the local legal community. Goodman won the cushy assignment for 1944 and thus found himself presiding over the trial of the twenty-six Tule Lake draft resisters. The defendants' court-appointed attorneys had persuaded the men to plead guilty, but Goodman refused to accept the plea and asked a former law school classmate who was practicing in Eureka to mount a serious defense. After hearing the defendants' testimony, Goodman concluded, "it is shocking to the conscience that an American citizen be confined...and then while under duress and restraint, be compelled to serve in the armed forces or be prosecuted for not yielding to such compulsion." Goodman dismissed the case, but fearing a hostile, even violent reaction from the local Eureka populace, he waited until the day he was scheduled to leave town before announcing the decision. The shocked prosecutors decided not to appeal, since the government had no plans to actually draft the Tule Lake "disloyals" in any event.

When Goodman assumed jurisdiction over *Abo v. Clark* in the spring of 1947, the case took on new life. On June 20, he ruled on the habeas corpus suit. He held that whatever the legal status of the renunciants might be, it was not "enemy alien," as defined by the Alien Enemies Act of 1798. He therefore ruled that the government had no legal authority to deport or incarcerate the plaintiffs. His order ended the specter of involuntary deportations and resulted in the freeing of the last renunciants held at Crystal Springs, Texas and Seabrook, New Jersey. Goodman's action also forced the government to create a new status for the renunciants. The Justice Department lawyers came up with the designation "native American alien." Although born in the United States, renunciants were defined as legal residents rather than citizens.

That changed on April 29, 1948, when Goodman issued his decision on *Abo v. Clark*. Since Congress had repealed Public Law 405, he did not rule on the issue of the statute's constitutionality. But on the renunciants' request for restoration of citizenship, Goodman handed Collins a complete victory. In remarkably similar language to his earlier decision in the draft resisters' case, Goodman said that it was "shocking to the conscience that an American citizen could be confined without authority and that while so under duress and restraint, for this government to accept a surrender of his constitutional heritage." Goodman described the atmosphere at Tule Lake as one of "fear, anxiety, resentment, uncertainty, hopelessness, and despair" that produced "mass hysteria." Under these circumstances, the government had "committed error" in accepting the renunciations. Goodman declared "the plaintiffs to be citizens of the United States."

The judge delayed issuing his order to allow the government to "designate individuals who were not affected by duress." To Collins's dismay, this process was drawn out for months. Finally, on February 25, 1949, the Justice Department presented the judge with a list of more than 3,500 names, nearly all the approximately 4,000 plaintiffs now in the case. Collins angrily objected, and Goodman essentially concurred. On May 2, 1949, the judge issued his final order, disregarding the Justice Department list and restoring American citizenship to all plaintiffs.

Judge Goodman's decision was Wayne Collins's greatest victory in his long legal battle to protect Nikkei rights. Although it was partially overturned on appeal, the decision established the validity of Collins's argument that renunciation of citizenship under duress was not voluntary and thus not legally binding. In a sense, the burden of proof had now shifted to the government to show that any renunciation decision was *not* made under duress.

Collins must have appreciated the congratulations from the Tule Lake Defense Committee, the Northern California branch of the ACLU, and many others. But not all the feedback was positive. One M. S. Parker, of Visalia, California, wrote Collins that "the Jap sympathizers seem to be still on the job....You know and I know that that bunch of perverted fanatics can't make good citizens." Collins responded that "inasmuch as your letter exhibits to me persistent ignorance...I suggest sometime that, if you are literate enough, you read the Constitution of the United States, as well as the Declaration of Independence, so as to learn what the rights of citizens are." Wayne Collins had not lost his combative spirit and that was going to serve him well in the nearly twenty years of legal battles that still lay ahead.

CHAPTER 6

CITIZENS

In some respects, A. L. (Al) Wirin was to the Southern California branch of the American Civil Liberties Union what Wayne Collins was to the Northern California branch: the go-to lawyer for important cases. Born in Russia, Wirin immigrated to the United States with his family when he was a child. He grew up in a Jewish immigrant neighborhood in Boston. In spite of his humble origins, he graduated from Harvard then from Boston University School of Law. After working for a time at the ACLU headquarters in New York, he moved to Southern California and became staff attorney for the Southern California branch. In 1934, while advocating on behalf of farm workers in the Imperial Valley, he was kidnapped and beaten by pro-grower vigilantes. If anything, this strengthened his commitment to civil liberties and social justice. Although he eventually established a private practice in Los Angeles, like Collins, he continued participating in ACLU cases. During the war, he served as counsel for the JACL, and we have already seen that in that capacity, wrote the Supreme Court amicus brief in the *Korematsu* and *Endo* cases.

Until late 1945, Wirin was on cordial terms with Wayne Collins and Ernest Besig. In October 1944, he wrote to Collins: "Drop me a note about your adventure before the Supreme Court." He later wrote approvingly about Eugene Rostow's article attacking the court's *Korematsu* ruling. On August 30, 1945, Wirin said that he and his fiancée were coming to San Francisco and suggested dinner with Collins, Besig, and their wives. The evening was apparently a success, for Wirin subsequently wrote Collins to thank him for an "unusually pleasant" time. But later that fall, Al Wirin became involved in a dispute over the renunciant cases that led to a permanent break with both Collins and Besig.

At about the same time that Collins was filing his first briefs in *Abo v. Clark* in November of 1945, Wirin was recruiting individual plaintiffs for his own renunciant case. He proposed that the two attorneys cooperate. He apparently told the *Pacific Citizen*, the newsletter of the JACL, that he was going to be one of the attorneys on the *Abo* case. Besig informed the *Citizen* that this was not true. The suit, he said, was filed by Wayne Collins "as a private attorney for the group with the full support of the American Civil Liberties Union of San Francisco" and without the participation of Al Wirin. The *Citizen* published the correction in its December 1 edition, and Wirin wrote Collins, asking him to set the record straight. Collins stood by Besig, telling Wirin, "I have never informed you that you were or that you would be associated with me in these cases." On February 14, 1946, Wirin wrote a letter to Besig, which implied that Besig and Collins were in the case for the money, that they were just trying to keep the $75,000 collected by the Tule Lake Defense Committee. Wirin told Besig, "I don't care to discuss the immigration cases with you any further; nor for that matter any other matter."

Wirin sent a copy of his letter to Roger Baldwin, probably hoping to win the support of the ACLU national office. Ever since the stockade conflict in 1944, Baldwin and the ACLU national board had tried to steer clear of the Tule Lake controversies. In August 1945, national board member, prominent civil libertarian, and Berkeley resident Alexander Meiklejohn wrote that he and attorney Charles Horsky believed that the renunciants were now "aliens" and that the question of their deportation was "administrative" rather than a matter of legal rights. Indeed, at least some of Meiklejohn's colleagues in the ACLU hierarchy favored deportation of "disloyal" renunciants. In reply, Besig criticized Meiklejohn for using the term "alien" and asked what federal statute gives the government the right to deport native born Americans. "It seems to me," Besig observed, "that our National [ACLU] Office relies too heavily on the opinion of its friends within the government," when, in fact, "it is the government actions that we are complaining about."

Roger Baldwin apparently suggested that the ACLU bring a test case regarding the government's authority to deport the renunciants as a compromise between Besig's and Meiklejohn's positions. But Besig rejected the idea. He believed that the government would deport virtually all of the renunciants by the time a test case regarding one or two individuals was decided. Besig continued to support Collins's class action suit, *Abo v. Clark*, to prohibit the deportation and reestablish the US citizenship of all renunciants. In the end, Baldwin prohibited spending any ACLU funds, either from the national office or the local branches, on renunciant cases. Presumably, Wayne Collins and Al Wirin both had to proceed without ACLU support.

This was not a problem for Collins, who was able to depend on financial and logistical support from the Tule Lake Defense

Committee. The committee urged renunciants to reject Wirin's offer and join the class action suit. In fact, several plaintiffs did just that, quitting Wirin's case and signing on with Collins. In the end, Wirin represented just three renunciants. A federal district judge in Los Angeles ruled in their favor, restoring their citizenship. In 1949 the Ninth Circuit Court of Appeals upheld the ruling. Collins and Besig believed that despite Baldwin's statement to the contrary, the national ACLU had supported Wirin's case representing three individual plaintiffs as a way of subverting *Abo v Clark*. Besig called Wirin "slippery," while Collins developed an "intense hostility toward Wirin."

In an interview more than fifty years after the fact, Tex Nakamura still talked of a Wirin-Baldwin conspiracy. There is no "smoking gun" that shows the conspiracy actually existed, and historian Greg Robinson doubts that Wirin would have been part of such a plot. But the fact that Collins and his colleagues sincerely believed that Baldwin and Wirin engaged in such conduct is an indication of the huge breach in trust that had developed between the Northern California branch and the national ACLU by late 1945. In March of 1946, Collins said, "there is no genuine American Civil Liberties Union...save and except the American Civil Liberties Union of Northern California."

Whether or not any conspiracy existed, Collins had grounds to be concerned about Wirin's case. Because he was pursuing a class action, Collins had to show that there was a common experience of duress suffered by all plaintiffs. He argued that the common theme was the policy of the United States government. By incarcerating Nisei citizens at Tule Lake and promoting or at least allowing terrible conditions to exist in the camp, the government made it impossible for anyone to make an informed, voluntary decision to renounce citizenship. Wirin, on the other hand, had only to show that his three clients suffered extreme duress. For example, he could argue that his clients were intimidated by the violence of the pro-Japan groups at Tule without having to show that all renunciants were so intimidated. Collins, in contrast, argued that the intimidation by what he called "government created fanatics" was part of a larger pattern of government conduct. Government policies had helped to create the "fanatics," and the government was unwilling or unable to protect Tule residents from the threats and violence of the pro-Japan organizations.

As we have seen, Judge Goodman accepted Collins's argument and ordered the government to restore the citizenship rights of all plaintiffs. But in its appeal of Judge Goodman's decision, the Justice Department lawyers argued for a more limited verdict. The government said that Goodman erred by not looking at the individual circumstances of the plaintiffs. Even if some had experienced extreme duress, others may have been in a situation that allowed a reasoned, voluntary decision. On January 17, 1951, the appeals court largely agreed. Writing for the court, Chief Judge William Denham upheld Goodman's decision to restore the citizenship of the approximately nine hundred plaintiffs who had been under twenty-one when they renounced. They had been minors and not qualified to make a choice of that magnitude. But Denham held that for competent adult plaintiffs, who eventually numbered more than four thousand, Goodman needed to examine each case individually and determine if the decision was made under duress or was entirely voluntary. Judge Denham and the appeals court had indeed shattered the class action. Wayne Collins now faced the prospect of arguing individual cases as Al Wirin had done. Only, for Collins this meant arguing the cases of four thousand separate plaintiffs.

Collins's one-man office could not have possibly handled four thousand renunciant cases. Even if he had somehow gathered an army of attorneys to share the load, the Tule Lake Defense Committee could not have raised enough money to support four thousand separate court actions. Fortunately, the Justice Department was also not prepared to take on this kind of caseload. With Judge Goodman's assistance, Collins and the government attorneys came up with a somewhat less burdensome procedure. Collins would submit an affidavit on behalf of each plaintiff. If the Justice Department had no evidence to contradict the facts of a particular affidavit, Judge Goodman would issue a court order restoring the person's citizenship. If the government did have specific objections, Collins could submit additional material on behalf of his client. Only if the lawyers could not eventually come to a mutual decision, would Goodman need to hold a formal court hearing.

Although it avoided the possibility of four thousand separate trials, the affidavit process put a substantial burden on Collins's small law office. Just finding the plaintiffs could take a tremendous amount of time and work. Once released from custody and given "native American alien" status, renunciants could live and work anywhere in the United States. They were also eligible for military service, and Collins estimated between two hundred and three hundred were in the armed forces, some fighting in Korea. Minoru Kiyota even served in US military intelligence in Japan and Korea while officially classified as a "native American alien." Once the plaintiff was found, the amount of paperwork required for each person was extensive. Collins filed at least ten thousand affidavits and follow-up documents with the Department of Justice, and that was after significant correspondence with the plaintiffs themselves.

Much of the administration of the affidavit process fell on the shoulders of Chiyo Wada, Collins's office secretary. Chiyo was the daughter of his old friend Senri Nao, and she had known Collins her whole life. She attended the University of California and met her future husband, Yori Wada, there in the late 1930s. He joined the army before the attack on Pearl Harbor and thus avoided removal to the camps. After her family was relocated to the Topaz, Utah, camp, the Office of War Information hired Chiyo Wada to work at its Denver facility as a Japanese language specialist. In September 1944, she wrote Collins to announce that she was expecting a baby. After the war, the young family returned to San Francisco. While Chiyo became Collins's secretary, Yori worked as a youth counselor and YMCA director, eventually becoming a prominent figure in San Francisco public life. In 1980 Governor Jerry Brown appointed Yori Wada as the first Asian American regent of the University of California.

As office secretary, Chiyo Wada contacted plaintiffs, prepared affidavits, and handled much of the correspondence involved in the complex renunciant legal process. Her competence in the Japanese language was key in dealing with Kibei plaintiffs who often had difficulty in English. She also directed, and probably helped recruit, several Nisei women and men who volunteered to assist with the vast amount of paperwork. Often the unpaid volunteers worked in the evening after regular office hours, typing letters and documents and engaging in other essential tasks. The volunteer efforts underscore once again that Wayne Collins was not rescuing helpless victims so much as creating a catalyst for plaintiff activism. He assisted the plaintiffs and their supporters in defending and exercising their rights as citizens of the United States. In 2015, more than half a century after the fact, the National Japanese American Historical Society honored several Nisei who had been active in the defense of the renunciants, including Chiyo Wada and former office volunteers Yoshie Handa Yasuda, Eiko Aoki, Sam Nao, Jean Kajikawa Sakai, and Florence Dobashi.

Over the course of the long legal process, the Tule Lake Defense Committee also played an increasingly important role in the renunciant cases. From its Southern California headquarters, the committee facilitated communication between the plaintiffs and Collins's office. The committee also recruited new participants in the case. Included were renunciants who had voluntarily relocated to Japan. Some of them found they could not return to the United States even to visit family because they no longer had an American (or Japanese) passport. There were also "strandees," American citizens who had been stranded in Japan when the war began and whose legal status was now unclear. Collins and the committee were able to negotiate an agreement with the government allowing renunciants and strandees to file documents supporting their affidavits at US consulates in Japan. The consulate staff would forward the papers to the Justice Department. By 1959, 1,327 renunciants living in Japan had recovered their citizenship and passports through the efforts of Collins and the Tule Lake Defense Committee.

One of the committee's major tasks was persuading plaintiffs to make their expected financial contribution to the defense fund. While no one was turned away for not paying, we have seen that the committee initially expected parties to the suit to contribute one hundred dollars to defray Collins's expenses. As those expenses grew during the affidavit process, the contribution amount was raised to three hundred dollars. The committee not only expected that new plaintiffs pay the three-hundred-dollar fee, but also asked old plaintiffs to pay another two hundred dollars to bring their total contribution up to the three-hundred-dollar figure. Some of the old-timers complained bitterly about the extra contribution. Collins tried to convince the California Bar Association to mediate the financial dispute. After studying the matter, the association declined to become involved.

Although the committee had no power to force plaintiffs to make contributions, it wasn't above trying to shame them into paying their fair share. In 1951, for example, the committee sent a letter to plaintiffs pointing out that "for six solid years, Mr. Collins has labored single-handed to protect and preserve our rights." The letter said that "thousands of dollars" had been spent on the legal fight. "No person in the case has the right to expect to take a free ride at the expense of the others who have met their share of the financial burden." Such appeals were effective. At the beginning of 1958, its last year of operation, the committee still had about $114,000 in its accounts. Nevertheless, Tex Nakamura and Collins were always concerned about freeloaders. In 1954, Nakamura told Collins about a renunciant in Japan who dropped out of the suit as soon as he received his American passport. The guy still owed $280, which he obviously was never going to pay. Nakamura wrote, "he is just a no good son of a gun."

Judge Denham's 1951 appeals court decision and the beginning of the affidavit process coincided with some of the high and low points of Wayne Collins's personal life. It was just a few months before the decision that Thelma and Wayne Collins moved their family into the newly purchased Presidio Avenue house. After years of living in rented apartments, Collins now owned his own home in a prestigious San Francisco neighborhood. His artist friend Bruce Porter helped the couple decorate their new home with heavy wood furniture and Japanese art from Senri Nao's shop. But the happy mood was soon destroyed by Thelma's cancer diagnosis. Her death three years later, in 1953, was a devastating blow for Collins and his children.

One of Collins's reactions to Thelma's passing seems have been to devote himself even more fully than before to his legal work. According to historian Donald E. Collins (no relation), during the renunciant years, Collins "maintained virtually a one-case office." But, in fact, he maintained a varied and active practice during the fifties and early sixties. In addition to the renunciant case, he did legal work for the Swedenborgian Church, handled family matters and then probate proceedings for his friends the Porters and Astaroth Haskell, and represented Senri Nao in business dealings. Collins also represented a Hong Kong businessman in a long-running dispute with the US Treasury Department and defended East Indian immigrants against possible deportation. And as we have seen, he represented several San Francisco educators who had been fired from their teaching jobs for refusing to answer California's anticommunist loyalty oath and defended Berkeley student demonstrators.

One case that was closely related to the renunciant dispute involved Japanese Peruvians incarcerated in the United States. During World War II, the US government encouraged Latin American countries with Japanese immigrant populations to establish prison camps similar to those in the United States. Instead of creating its own facilities, Peru deported about 1,700 Japanese Peruvians to the United States. They were imprisoned in the Justice Department immigration facility at Crystal City, Texas. The US government may have eventually traded some of the Japanese Peruvians for American citizens imprisoned in Japan. After the war, Peru refused to admit most of the Japanese immigrants back into the country. The US Department of Justice designated them as "enemy aliens" and ordered them deported to Japan. Some accepted Japanese repatriation, and the Peruvian government finally allowed a handful of people who had Peruvian citizenship back into the country. But about three hundred of the Japanese Peruvians wished to remain in the United States.

Collins and Nakamura first encountered the Peruvians in 1945 while visiting Tule Lake renunciants, whom the government had also imprisoned in Crystal City. With the support of the Tule Lake Defense Committee, Collins agreed to represent the three hundred Peruvians who applied for US residency. According to one account, when Collins first contacted the Justice Department about the Japanese Peruvians, a department lawyer said to a colleague, "Uh-oh, Collins has found them." In 1946, Collins instituted habeas corpus proceedings to free his Peruvian clients from custody and prevent their deportation. The government agreed to suspend the deportations but then classified the Japanese Peruvians as illegal aliens, still subject to removal from the United States. Collins pointed out that if his clients were in the United States illegally, it was because the government broke the law by bringing them into the country in the first place. Eventually, the Justice Department reclassified the remaining Japanese Peruvians in the United States as resident aliens and allowed them to stay. In 1952, Congress passed a new immigration law, which finally permitted Asian immigrants to become naturalized American citizens. Several of the Japanese Peruvians joined some long-time Issei residents in taking advantage of the new legislation.

After some procedural delay following the 1951 appellate court ruling, Collins began the renunciant affidavit process in earnest in 1953. At first it was slow going, with the Justice Department objecting to most of the plaintiffs' claims. In 1955, the pace of approvals picked up, and during the following year the Justice Department announced a "liberalized policy" regarding the affidavits. The policy modification reflected deeper changes in American politics and society. It had been ten years since the war ended, and the Eisenhower administration now saw Japan as an important Cold War ally, not an enemy. The Supreme Court's 1954 *Brown v. Board of Education* decision and the 1955 Montgomery Bus Boycott heralded the beginning of the Civil Rights Movement and a new assault on segregation and discrimination. Scholarly works on the Nikkei removal and incarceration published in the 1950s were generally critical of Executive Order 9066 and the *Korematsu* decision. In 1958 US Assistant Attorney General George C. Doub said the wartime treatment of Japanese Americans "constituted a tragic failure of principle by the executive power in accomplishing it and of the judicial power in sustaining it."

In this transformed political environment, the trickle of affidavit approvals became a steady stream and then a modest flood. Collins began sending the Tule Lake Defense Committee long lists of people whose citizenship had been restored. On February 7, 1957, Judge Goodman issued an order recognizing the citizenship of Tadayasu Abo, the plaintiff for whom the *Abo v. Clark* case was named. Goodman's order stated that legally Abo had never lost his citizenship, despite Justice Department actions and statements to the contrary. Collins wrote Abo that he had no reason to be ashamed of his past renunciation. The government had "taken advantage of you while it held you under duress and deprived you of practically all the rights of citizenship."

On May 22, 1957, the governing board of the Tule Lake Defense Committee wrote Collins that the committee would cease its operations on March 31, 1958. Given the pace of Justice Department approvals, the committee leadership assumed that virtually all the renunciant cases would be favorably resolved by that date. The committee proposed that Collins and Tex Nakamura use any funds left in the defense accounts after March 31 to carry on individual cases that remained unresolved. In the meantime, the committee said it would make a "final effort" to get any missing information from remaining plaintiffs in Japan. After discussing other proce dural details, the board members closed the letter by thanking Collins "for all that you have done for the plaintiff-renunciants."

On May 20, 1959, the Department of Justice held a ceremony in Washington, DC, to celebrate the completion of its "program of restitution of citizenship." Attorney General William P. Rogers explained that the renunciations were the "result of a wave of bitterness and hysteria." Rogers proudly announced that citizenship had been restored to 4,978 of the 5,409 people who requested restoration, an acceptance rate of over 90 percent. Among those attending the event was Eugene Rostow, now dean of the Yale Law School and recognized for his early criticism of the *Korematsu* decision.

Another honored guest was Edward Ennis, the former head of the Justice Department's Alien Enemy Control Unit, who had already played important, if contradictory, roles in the Nikkei cases. After leaving government service, Ennis became the general counsel for the national American Civil Liberties Union, which had of course flatly refused to assist the renunciants in 1945. While at the Justice Department, Ennis had told renunciants they would be deported and that there was no possibility of recovering their citizenship. But addressing the 1959 ceremony as ACLU general counsel, Ennis explained that the renunciations had been caused not by disloyalty, but "by the shock of the special evacuation treatment...and of course by the incredible condition of confusion and terror prevailing at Tule Lake." The world had definitely turned. Wayne Collins may not have been honored at the ceremony, but it seemed as if official Washington was now paraphrasing his legal briefs and repeating his moral arguments.

The federal government was not the only American institution that had changed its position by 1959. During the war, the Hearst newspaper chain had been one of the most ferocious proponents of the removal and incarceration program. Yet on May 22, 1959, the *San Francisco Examiner*, a Hearst paper, ran an editorial praising the Justice Department's settlement of the renunciant cases. The paper agreed with Attorney General Rogers that "our country did make a mistake" in imprisoning the Nikkei. The editorial said that the effect of that act on "the lives of the American citizens involved can never be fully compensated." Yet none of this was good enough for Wayne Collins. Even after the attorney general's action, there were still some four hundred plaintiffs who had not recovered their citizenship. Collins spent the next nine years clearing these remaining cases.

On March 6, 1968, Collins withdrew the name of Tukuji Nakamoto, the last remaining plaintiff in the *Abo* case. Nakamoto apparently could not be found and his name was dropped "without prejudice" so that his claim could be renewed if he reappeared. This effectively ended the renunciant case twenty-three years after Collins filed his initial brief. Judge Goodman had died in 1961, and Judge Alfonso Zirpoli had taken over the case. As a young federal lawyer in 1942, Zirpoli had been the prosecuting attorney in the *Korematsu* case, arguing against Wayne Collins in federal district court. Now he presided over the termination of *Abo*, probably the longest legal battle produced by Executive Order 9066. When Collins initiated the *Abo* case in 1945, Tom Clark was attorney general of the United States. In 1968, when the *Abo* case finally came to an end, Tom Clark's son Ramsey Clark served as attorney general.

Judge Zirpoli graciously allowed Wayne Collins to have the last word. In a "Statement of Counsel for Plaintiffs Canceling Cases," Collins said that each plaintiff was an American citizen who had been imprisoned "simply because each had ancestors who once were inhabitants of the country known as Japan." They were treated as enemy aliens because "under government duress they purportedly renounced their citizenship." Now, the renunciations "have been cancelled for having been unconstitutional.... The fundamental rights, liberties, privileges and immunities of these citizens now are honored." Collins concluded that, "the episode which constituted an infamous chapter in our history has come to an end." But Wayne Collins's participation in the Nikkei cases had not yet come to an end. In 1968, he was still trying to overturn the conviction of Iva Toguri D'Aquino, aka Tokyo Rose.

CHAPTER 7

"TOKYO ROSE"

After Wayne Collins's death in July of 1974, the *New York Times* published an obituary entitled "Wayne Collins, 74, Tokyo Rose Lawyer." A longer obit in the *San Francisco Chronicle* identified Collins as "the fiery little lawyer who defended Tokyo Rose." The Tokyo Rose treason trial, which began in the summer of 1949 and lasted three months, may have cost the government as much as $700,000 ($7 million in today's dollars). At the time, it was the longest and most expensive federal court case in the Ninth Circuit and perhaps in the country. It certainly was Collins's highest profile case and the one for which he was best known by the general public. The irony is that his client, Iva Toguri D'Aquino, was not then nor never had been "Tokyo Rose." As Collins's associate in the case, George Olshausen, put it, "professional Jap-haters" had seized upon the "legend of Tokyo Rose…expanded it, promoted it, and climactically produced a victim in the person of Iva D'Aquino."

Iva Toguri was born in Los Angeles in 1916. Her Japanese immigrant parents established a reasonably prosperous mercantile business in Southern California, and Iva grew up in a middle class household. As a child, she had many white friends and claimed never to have experienced discrimination. She attended Compton Junior College and graduated from UCLA with a bachelor's degree in zoology. In the summer of 1941, she went to Japan for the first time in her life to help care for an aunt who was ill. Like some travelers of that era, she did not wait to get a passport but instead traveled with a notarized "certificate of identity" which confirmed her American citizenship.

With only a rudimentary knowledge of the Japanese language, Toguri found it difficult to adjust to life in Japan. She wrote her siblings, "no matter how bad things get and how much you have to take in forms of racial criticism, and how hard you have to work, by all means remain [in the United States]." In September, she applied for an American passport to facilitate her return to the US. The passport had not arrived by November. When she attempted to book passage home, she was informed her certificate of identity was not sufficient proof of her American citizenship. War broke out between Japan and the United States on December 7, and Iva Toguri found herself stranded in Japan.

Despite her circumstance, Toguri did not hide her belief that the United States would and should win the war. Her presence in her aunt's home became so embarrassing for the family that she had to move to a rented room. She was watched and often visited by Japanese security agents who tried to persuade her to renounce her American citizenship and declare allegiance to Japan. Toguri refused, not only keeping her status as a US citizen, but also declining to buy Japanese war bonds. She claimed the security agents told her that the only reason she was not interned along with other enemy citizens was that it would be a waste of valuable resources for the government to feed her. She was barely able to support herself by teaching English and working part time for the Danish legation. She also found work as typist at the Dōmei News Agency, where she met Felipe D'Aquino, a Portuguese citizen of Japanese and Portuguese parentage. He spoke good English and shared her pro-Allied sentiments. The two eventually married, Iva giving up her family's Methodist faith and converting to Catholicism.

In the summer of 1943, Toguri went to work at Radio Tokyo, typing scripts for English language broadcasts. There she met three Allied prisoners of war who Japanese authorities had forced to produce propaganda programs aimed at reducing the morale and fighting spirit of American and Australian servicemen in the Pacific. The leader of the POW group was Major Charles Cousens, of the Australian Imperial Force, an experienced broadcaster who had been captured in Singapore. The group also included a US Army captain, Wallace Ince, and a Filipino lieutenant, Norman Reyes, both of whom had become Japanese prisoners after the surrender of Corregidor in the Philippines. All three had experienced brutality in Japanese prisoner of war camps and were barely surviving on what amounted to a starvation diet. Toguri began surreptitiously supplying them with food and medicines.

In the fall of 1943, Cousens decided to use Iva as a disc jockey for a program called *The Zero Hour*, which was broadcast in English five or six days a week from 6:00 to 7:00 p.m., Tokyo time. Initially, she refused, but Cousens privately assured her there would be no political content to her performances. Indeed, he promised the scripts would subtly undermine the propaganda with humor. Colonel Shigetsugu Tsuneishi, head of English language programing at Radio Tokyo, made it clear that Iva had no choice in the matter. She was ordered to become an announcer on *The Zero Hour*.

Iva Toguri joined at least a dozen other female English language on-air personalities on Radio Tokyo. By 1942, well over a year before Toguri began broadcasting, Allied servicemen in the Pacific were calling any and all of these women "Tokyo Rose." It was a nickname and character invented by listeners rather than a title used by Radio Tokyo or the women broadcasters. But Iva was the only one of the group who insisted on keeping her American citizenship. This meant that only she would eventually be prosecuted for treason. As Japanese citizens, the other women were simply serving their country much as an enemy soldier serves his. Ironically, Toguri's very loyalty to the United States put her in a position to be prosecuted for alleged disloyalty by the United States government.

Toguri's chosen on-air name was Orphan Ann, based on the popular comic-strip character Little Orphan Annie. Iva mainly cracked lame jokes, engaged in light banter, and introduced recorded American popular music. Only a few of her scripts and recordings were recovered after the war, but none of them contain any political content, let alone anti-American or pro-Japanese commentary. On March 9, 1944, for example, she asked her listeners to be an "Orphan Choir" and sing along with the music. After the record finished, she commented "That's not bad atoll, atoll…alright boys, one more lap, and then you can have your beer…what no beer? Well what sort of a war is this? Never mind, sing first, and write to (Secretary of the Interior) Ickes afterwards. Maybe he'll run a pipe for you…sing, sing, little ones!"

Toguri appeared on *The Zero Hour* six days a week from November 1943 to May 1944 and then five days a week from May 1944 until the end of the war in August 1945. Shortly after the Japanese surrender, two American journalists, Clark Lee with International News Service and Harry Brundidge of *Cosmopolitan* magazine, came to Japan with the idea of finding the "real" Tokyo Rose. A Japanese intermediary put them in touch with Iva, and she signed a contract with Brundidge allowing him to tell her story in return for a payment of two thousand dollars. In the contract she agreed that she was "the one and original Tokyo Rose." This was, of course, untrue, but two thousand dollars was an enormous sum of money in the devastated physical and social environment of postwar Japan. In any event, she never collected the money and Brundidge never published his story in *Cosmopolitan*. Clark Lee moved on to other projects, but Brundidge continued to claim he had found Tokyo Rose. His obsession was to play a major part in Iva's eventual prosecution.

Brundidge's claim that Toguri was Tokyo Rose probably had something to do with her arrest by the US Army in October of 1945. She was held without charge in Tokyo while first the army and then the Justice Department investigated her wartime activities. Eventually, they concluded Toguri had not violated any laws, and she was released in October of 1946. She became pregnant in 1947. Determined that her child would be born in the United States, in October of that year Iva again applied for an American passport. Although the baby died at birth, Toguri continued to pursue a return to her home country. By that time, much of the American public had heard the story of the so-called Tokyo Rose, and Iva's passport request set off a round of protests. The commander of the American Legion and the officers of the Native Sons of the Golden West were among those denouncing her as a traitor.

The campaign against Tokyo Rose became especially serious when Walter Winchell joined the cause. He was a newspaper and broadcast gossip columnist, and his radio program was one of the most popular in the country. In response to Winchell's criticism of the Justice Department, Attorney General Tom Clark ordered a review of Toguri's case. Justice Department officials, accompanied by journalist Harry Brundidge, traveled to Japan in March of 1948 to interview Iva once again. The government later learned that while in Japan, Brundidge attempted to bribe two Japanese nationals to testify against Iva. In the end, department lawyers again recommended against prosecuting. But Attorney General Clark apparently believed the government had to act. He referred the matter to Thomas De Wolfe, a Justice Department lawyer who had won treason convictions against German sympathizers. De Wolfe also concluded there was insufficient evidence to warrant prosecution. But Clark was not to be denied. In August 1948, he ordered De Wolfe to proceed with the case against Iva Toguri D'Aquino, the so-called Tokyo Rose.

Toguri was arrested once again and transported by ship to San Francisco. She arrived under guard on September 25, 1948, returning to the United States for the first time in more than seven years, though not exactly in the manner she had planned. Prosecutor Thomas De Wolfe brought the case before a federal grand jury in San Francisco. De Wolfe had a difficult time convincing some members of the jury; he said he had to "practically make a Fourth of July speech." In the end, however, the grand jury handed down an indictment, listing eight overt acts of treason. Most of them were remarkably bland and imprecise. "Overt Act I," for example, charged that the defendant "discussed with another person the proposed participation of defendant in the radio broadcasting program." "Overt Act VIII" charged the defendant with engaging " in an entertainment dialogue with an employee of the Broadcasting

Corporation of Japan for radio purposes." "Overt Act VI" was the most specific, saying the defendant "did speak into a microphone concerning the loss of ships."

While Toguri had spent the war in Japan, her family was imprisoned at the Gila River camp in Arizona. Her mother died during the war, and her father, Jun Toguri, eventually moved the rest of the family to Chicago, where they operated a successful gift store. When Iva arrived in San Francisco in 1948, she saw her father for the first time since she had left Los Angeles for Japan in 1941. Jun assured her of the family's support, telling her "I'm proud of you. You didn't change your stripes." Of her family, Iva later said, "It would have been much easier for them if they had abandoned me. They haven't. They stuck by me."

Jun Toguri began looking for a lawyer to defend his daughter and inevitably contacted Wayne Collins, who was well known in the Japanese American community because of his work on the *Korematsu* and renunciant cases. Collins agreed to take Iva Toguri's case *pro bono*, at no cost to the family. Eventually, Jun did pay some of the travel expenses related to the case, but Collins ended up representing Iva for more than two decades basically without charge. After Collins's death, his son Wayne Merrill Collins served as her attorney for another three years on the same basis. All told, the Collins family, father and son, generously donated more than a quarter century of free legal service to the Toguris.

In 1948, realizing the enormity of the Tokyo Rose case and already burdened with the renunciant legal proceedings, Collins brought on two associates to help him represent Iva Toguri. Both were established San Francisco lawyers who had worked with Collins in the past. Politically, they were an odd couple: Theodore

Tamba was a conservative Republican who eventually made a good living representing insurance companies, while George Olshausen was a radical who regularly contributed articles to the *Independent Socialist Review*. Like Collins, both men agreed to serve without compensation. Tamba explained, "I hate to see the Government kick little people around. I'm a Republican, and I believe in the Constitution of the United States, and I don't like a Democratic Administration kicking people around." Olshausen believed that "the trial was political...taking it as a strictly legal matter, they butchered her."

US District Judge Michael Joseph Roche presided over the case. Roche was born in Ireland and immigrated to the United States with his family when he was a child. He had served as municipal judge in San Francisco for twenty-five years before President Roosevelt appointed him to the federal bench in 1935. He was seventy-one years old at the time of the Tokyo Rose trial and sometimes dozed off during the proceedings. He was known as the "jovial judge," but that was not the way Collins saw him. In his trial rulings and comments, Roche seemed to favor the prosecution, consistently limiting the scope of Collins's defense. In an interview with journalists Katherine Pinkham and Rex Gunn, given nearly a decade after the trial, Roche admitted he might not have been completely objective: "I always felt there was something peculiar about that girl going to Japan when she did. I always thought she might have been up to something."

Thomas De Wolfe and his prosecution team had a major problem in arguing their case. Toguri's alleged "overt acts" of treason were in fact not physical acts, but words. And there was no physical evidence that those words existed. None of the surviving scripts or recordings of the *Zero Hour* programs covered the material included in the indictment. De Wolfe presented the testimony of former servicemen who claimed to have heard the programs, but five-year-old memories of broadcasts casually heard were hardly definitive. De Wolfe therefore had to rely on people who worked directly on the programs at Radio Tokyo. In effect, the case against Iva rested heavily on the testimony of employees of an enemy government. Department of Justice attorneys and FBI agents interviewed several possible witnesses in Japan. The US government flew those who agreed to testify to San Francisco, housing and feeding them at the Hotel Whitcomb on Market Street, and giving them ten dollars per diem for expenses. For residents of war-torn Japan, this could be an attractive offer. Wayne Collins believed that "Every son of a bitch who ever set foot in Radio Tokyo was willing to testify [against Iva Toguri] for a free plane ride and $10 per diem."

Collins and his defense team had far fewer resources to devote to finding Japanese witnesses. Judge Roche allocated three thousand dollars in federal funds for Theodore Tamba to travel to Japan but included no money for a translator. Tex Nakamura of the Tule Lake Defense Committee volunteered to accompany Tamba, with Jun Toguri paying Nakamura's travel expenses. Tamba and Nakamura found that the FBI had already spoken to many potential witnesses and that most of them feared they would face US government retribution if they cooperated with the Toguri defense. In the end, Collins chose to bring only Felipe D'Aquino from Japan, again with Jun Toguri paying travel costs.

The US government allowed D'Aquino into the country only if he signed a document agreeing to leave after the trial and never return to the United States. D'Aquino strongly defended his wife in his testimony, but Judge Roche refused to let him discuss the effect of the loss of the baby on Iva's state of mind. During the proceedings, D'Aquino often sat in the courtroom with the Toguri family. After the trial, he returned to Japan. Although they did not formally divorce, the couple never saw each other again. Speaking of her husband more than two decades later, Iva said, "Poor guy—he went through hell too....Losing the baby and Phil—it was unbearable. That's one of the reasons I have avoided thinking about it all these years....You can't bring back thirty years."

The trial began in a San Francisco federal courtroom on July 5, 1949. De Wolfe presented the testimony of former servicemen claiming to have heard the *Zero Hour* broadcasts. All swore they heard the programs at 6:00 p.m., which was the time of the Tokyo broadcasts. Collins pointed out that since some of the witnesses served in areas with different time zones than Tokyo, the broadcasts would have been received at various different times. It was also not clear that the witnesses had heard Toguri rather than one of the other female broadcasters. Most of the witnesses were unable to verify the exact date of particular programs, though one former sailor produced a dated copy of a letter he wrote to his wife on the day of a broadcast.

Colonel Shigetsugu Tsuneishi, head of Radio Tokyo's English-language program, testified that Toguri's job on *The Zero Hour* was to weaken the enemy's morale and fighting spirit. But since Tsuneishi could not speak English, he could not testify about what Iva actually said during the broadcasts. For this, the prosecution had to rely on two of Tsuneishi's assistants, George Mitsushio and Ken Oki. Both men were Nisei who had moved to Japan before the war and assumed Japanese citizenship. They testified that in an October 1944 broadcast, Toguri had mentioned the sinking of American ships and said, "Orphans of the Pacific. You are really orphans now. How will you get home, now that all your ships are sunk."

On cross-examination, Collins wondered how both men could remember the exact same words, five years after the fact. He asked Oki if he could remember what he had for breakfast that day five years ago or what the weather was like. He made sure the jury understood that the men were turncoats. He asked Mitsushio, a former University of California ROTC cadet, to recite the Pledge of Allegiance. Collins didn't know it at the time, but his suspicions about the two men were correct. In 1976, Mitsushio and Oki admitted that they had lied at the 1949 trial. They told the Tokyo correspondent of the *Chicago Tribune*, "We were told what to say and what not to say two hours every morning for a month before the trial started....If we didn't cooperate Uncle Sam might arrange a trial for us, too."

De Wolfe could not let Harry Brundidge testify without opening up the issue of his bribing potential witnesses. But the prosecution did call Clark Lee to testify about the journalists' initial 1945 discussions with Toguri and her signing a contract saying that she was "the one and original Tokyo Rose." Collins was able to establish the fact that there was no single person called by that name. He also tried to use the Lee testimony to open up the issue of Brundidge's bribery attempt. But Judge Roche sustained De Wolfe's objection and limited Collins's ability to bring up an issue that might have tainted the prosecution's case.

Collins maintained that Toguri was a loyal American who was not guilty of any of the overt acts alleged by the prosecution.

Continuing an argument he had used in the renunciant cases, Collins said Iva had agreed to do the broadcasts "under duress." In spite of that fact, Iva had given aid and comfort not to the Japanese government, but to Allied POWs. Collins presented the testimony of American veterans who claimed the broadcasts were "just entertainment" and had no effect on morale. Judge Roche refused to let Collins put into the record a humorous "Navy citation" issued by American sailors in August of 1945, thanking Tokyo Rose for "contributing greatly to the morale of American forces."

The testimony of the three prisoners of war with whom Toguri had worked was key to the defense case. Charles Cousens testified that he considered her a soldier under his command and that he would never let her express treasonous material. Although Judge Roche generally tried to limit testimony regarding Iva's assistance to the POWs, he did allow Cousens to describe some of her efforts on his behalf. When De Wolfe asked Cousens "did any other Japanese bring you food besides the defendant," Cousens reminded the prosecutor, "the defendant was not Japanese. She was American." Judge Roche also limited testimony about the brutality suffered by American prisoners of war, though he did permit Wallace Ince to describe a terrible beating he suffered at the hands of Japanese soldiers. Ince broke down in court while speaking of his ordeal. Norman Reyes also defended Iva's loyalty, but unbeknownst to Collins, Reyes had previously given a statement to the FBI supporting the government's case. When confronted with the conflict, Reyes claimed FBI agents had threatened him with prosecution unless he cooperated with the government. Tex Nakamura believed that Reyes's contradictory testimony was disastrous to the defense cause.

The defense's most important witness was Iva Toguri

D'Aquino. When she first appeared in court, Toguri's appearance surprised many observers. The stereotypical image of Tokyo Rose was a sexy, sophisticated siren, somewhat like the Dragon Lady, a character in the then popular comic strip *Terry and the Pirates*. Iva was short and dressed in neat but plain clothes. Although in person she could be talkative and assertive, her demeanor at the trial was quiet, serious, and unemotional. She later described her mood as being in something like a stunned trance. She answered Collins's questions clearly, telling the story of her difficult life in Japan. She denied making any of the statements alleged by the prosecution and of intentionally doing or saying anything disloyal to the United States. She said she had no choice but to become Orphan Ann. Above all, her aim had been to maintain her American citizenship and return to her home country.

After Collins's questions, Thomas De Wolfe subjected the witness to a withering cross-examination. De Wolfe's tone and manner were aggressive, hostile, and sarcastic. Toguri continued her unemotional demeanor, answering the questions calmly and remaining consistent with her original testimony. After eight days on the stand, Collins asked her a final question: "Do you still want to be an American citizen? " She answered, "Yes...that's why I made all those applications." And then the emotional dam broke and she began sobbing on the witness stand.

According to Stanton Delaplane, a Pulitzer Prize–winning reporter who covered the trial for the *San Francisco Chronicle*, most observers who sat through the thirteen weeks of testimony assumed the government had not made its case. Paine Knickerbocker of the *Oakland Tribune* had earlier written that the government's case "shows a basic weakness—no evidence exists." Among the ten reporters who covered the trial, the informal vote in favor of acquittal was 9 to 1. But Judge Roche's instructions to the jury directly attacked much of the defense argument. Roche said that even if the jury concluded that Toguri sincerely wanted to help the POWs, jurors could not consider that in their decision on the treason charges. Regarding the claim of duress, the judge said the jury could only consider if Iva faced threats of immediate death or physical injury, not the possibility of imprisonment or long-term retribution. After the trial, jury foreman John Mann said he believed the jury would have acquitted Toguri "if it had been possible under the judge's instructions."

The case went to the jurors on September 26, 1949. The jury consisted of six men and six women. All were white, as the prosecution objected to each of the black and Asian American people on the original jury panel. John Mann was an accountant from Oakland. He said a majority of jurors originally favored acquittal, but two jury members argued strongly in favor of a guilty verdict. Eventually, the group divided 9 to 3 in favor of conviction. After two days, Mann, one of the three-member minority, told the court the jury was hopelessly deadlocked and unable to reach a unanimous verdict. The defense believed a hung jury was tantamount to a victory, since the prosecution was unlikely to devote the time and money to retry the case. Judge Roche refused to end the trial, claiming that given the great expense to both sides, the jury had a duty to render a verdict. After two more days of difficult deliberation, Mann and his two allies gave in. On September 29, the jury found Iva not guilty of seven of the eight alleged overt acts. But the jurors found her guilty of Act VI, the accusation regarding sunken ships, and thus convicted Iva of treason. According to journalist

Rex Gunn, the alternate juror, who had sat through the whole trial but could not participate in the deliberations, said of the guilty verdict: "How could they do it? How could they possibly do it?"

If the verdict was surprising to many, the sentence handed down by Judge Roche on October 6, 1949 was shocking. The judge sentenced Toguri to ten years in federal prison and a fine of ten thousand dollars. In addition, conviction of treason automatically deprived Iva of her American citizenship. She would have been far better off if she had listened to the Japanese agents and agreed to renounce her citizenship back in 1942. Given the harsh sentence, John Mann was conscience-stricken that he had not held his ground. He told Gunn, "She may have done something wrong, but the Government didn't prove it. From a legal standpoint, the Government failed to convict her." Collins described the verdict as "the American Dreyfus Case minus only Devils Island."

Ever since she had arrived in the United States, Toguri had been held in the San Francisco County Jail. She counseled other inmates and helped serve breakfast every morning before going to court. She soon won the friendship and support of jail matrons and guards. This was also true of Bailiff Herbert Cole, who saw her each day in court. Cole had taken custody of Iva when she first arrived in San Francisco. After the verdict, it was his duty to transport her by train to the federal women's prison in West Virginia where she would serve her sentence. As Cole told Gunn, "I took her off the boat, and my wife and I took her to Alderson Prison in West Virginia. There was no criminal element about her—nothing at all."

At Alderson Toguri was the consummate model prisoner. At various times, she served as a supply clerk, medical aide, medical purchaser, and lab assistant. She seems to have ended up basically running the X-ray lab. After she was released early for good behavior in 1956, one wonders how the prison kept on operating. But release from prison did not end Iva's problems with the US government. A government immigration officer met her at the prison gate and informed her that as a noncitizen, she was scheduled for deportation in thirty days. Once again, Iva Toguri turned to Wayne Collins for help.

In San Francisco, Collins immediately instituted an appeal of the immigration order. Former jury foreman John Mann was among those writing letters in support of the appeal. While the process dragged on for months, Toguri lived in the Collins home on Presidio Avenue as a virtual member of the family. Wayne Merrill, who was eleven years old when she moved in, particularly remembers her helping him with his homework. He doubts he would have passed junior high school math if it hadn't been for Iva. She volunteered in Collins's law office; her duties probably included working with Chiyo Wada, processing paperwork for the renunciant cases. Finally, in July of 1958, the government ruled in favor of the appeal and allowed Iva to remain in the United States as a "native American alien." She had lost her citizenship, but at least she could live out her life in the United States.

Toguri joined her family in Chicago and eventually managed the store her father had started after the war. Collins had appealed the original verdict, but both the Ninth Circuit Court of Appeals and the US Supreme Court allowed the conviction to stand. In 1954, Theodore Tamba had petitioned for executive clemency and in 1968, Collins asked for an executive pardon, but Presidents Dwight Eisenhower and Lyndon Johnson declined to act. Collins also represented Toguri in negotiations regarding the ten-thousand-dollar fine. He was unable to prevent the government from seizing her life insurance policy as partial payment. Jun Toguri had offered to pay his daughter's fine, but during his lifetime, Iva refused to let him do so. After Jun's death in 1972, she discovered that his will contained a bequest to pay off the remaining amount owed to the government.

In 1974, Dave Ushio, executive director of the Japanese American Citizens League, dropped into Collins's office to discuss Toguri's case. Back in the late forties the JACL leadership was at best dismissive and at worst actively hostile to the woman they were more than willing to call Tokyo Rose. But now a new generation of leaders was taking another look at the case. Edison Uno, one of the most outspoken members of the new generation, had submitted a resolution regarding Iva to the annual JACL convention. The resolution contained an apology for the organization's former hostility and offered assistance in the future. Collins was not impressed and expressed his well-known contempt for the JACL, which he said still stood for "jackal." But Ushio argued back, pointing out that "I was just a kid when you had your trial." He told Collins that perhaps "if you had presented a better case, Iva wouldn't need a pardon now."

Collins finally agreed to set up a conversation between Ushio and Toguri, but the initial results were not promising. Iva basically told Ushio he was thirty years too late. Nevertheless, that first conversation began a process that eventually led to a full presidential pardon for Iva Toguri D'Aquino. Unfortunately, Collins was not able to enjoy the victory. In July of 1974, not long after his meeting with Ushio, Wayne Collins died of a heart attack.

CHAPTER 8

PASSING

In 1972, the California Historical Society presented *Executive Order 9066*, an exhibit of sixty-five War Relocation Authority photographs of the initial removal and incarceration of the Nikkei in 1942. Included in the exhibit were twenty-seven pictures taken by the noted documentary photographer Dorothea Lange. Lange and her husband, University of California professor Paul Taylor, were passionately opposed to the president's executive order and incarceration policy. Yet the WRA, in an act of profound bureaucratic ignorance, hired Dorothea Lange as one of its photographers. Her pictures particularly showed the suffering of the Nikkei, so much so that the government suppressed the images for more than two decades. *Executive Order 9066* opened in January of 1972 in San Francisco and Berkeley. It traveled throughout the country, and there were prominent showings in New York, Washington, and Chicago. The photographs and accompanying text had a significant impact on public opinion and helped pave the way for the redress movement, which eventually won monetary reparations for the victims of the executive order.

Nisei activist Edison Uno wrote the introduction to the exhibit's impressive catalogue, and historical society director J. S. Holliday asked him to suggest someone who might write the volume's epilogue. Uno mentioned several candidates and then said, "If you want to get an ear full, call or visit a S.F. attorney, Wayne Collins. He will write you a conclusion that printers will not print. If you haven't met Mr. Collins, you haven't experienced the bitterness of 110,000 evacuees in one fighting Irishman."

The historical society eventually chose former attorney general and supreme court justice Tom Clark to write the epilogue. It was a curious choice, given Clark's role in promoting the prosecutions of Fred Korematsu and Iva Toguri D'Aquino and the deportation of renunciants. But Uno's description of the elderly Wayne Collins was not entirely inaccurate. Dean Lipton, a San Francisco journalist who knew Collins well during his later years and greatly admired him for his "love for justice," also commented on Collins's unforgiving nature and willingness to hold a grudge. Lipton described a man who could be distant and difficult to know. Collins, he said, "remained a mystery to those of us who may have known him best."

By the late sixties, when Wayne Collins was himself in his late sixties, he was a somewhat solitary figure. His children had long since left home. Margaret lived three thousand miles away in New York State, and relations between Collins and his son, Wayne Merrill, were often difficult. In June of 1967, the elder Collins wrote Margaret that he hadn't seen his son "in some time." In August of 1968, Collins again remarked on Wayne Merrill's absence. Collins speculated that his son was "probably in Berkeley engaged in some sort of politicking." By this time, many of Collins's oldest friends, including Bruce Porter, Astaroth Haskell, and Senri Nao, had died, and he had fallen out with other friends like Ernest Besig.

Collins admitted he was not inclined "to forgive and forget." In 1971, he still held a grudge against the national office of the

American Civil Liberties Union. He told historian Donald Collins (no relation) that Al Wirin and Roger Baldwin had been "treacherous and endeavored to have my cases aborted." Four years earlier, Wayne Collins had rebuffed a conciliatory gesture by the Japanese American Citizens League. In 1967, Wesley T. Dui, chair of the JACL Banquet Committee, had invited Collins to a dinner honoring him and other "friends of the Japanese American community." Collins began his reply by politely declining the invitation. Then he told Dui that, "I hold and expect to hold during my lifetime hostility toward the Japanese American Citizens League." Collins said he believed "that the JACL would be doing the members of our population of immediate or remote Japanese ancestry a service were it to disband and disperse."

But Dr. Clifford Uyeda, like Edison Uno a member of a new generation of Nisei leaders, believed that beneath Collins's "fierce exterior," there was "a gentle humanitarian of great sensitivity." Uyeda said that Collins was a "fearless crusader" but also a "compassionate person and a tender loving man." Granted these words were written six years after Collins's death, when time might have softened the reputation of a sometimes angry and bitter man, but even in old age, Collins displayed many of the humanitarian qualities that Uyeda described.

Fighting the renunciant cases in the fifties and sixties, Collins had found that his clients were often ashamed of the fact that they had renounced their citizenship. He tried to restore their confidence and feeling of self-worth, telling them: "The government took advantage of you while you were held in duress." In 1971, more than a decade after his citizenship was restored, former renunciant Hiroshi Kashiwagi sent Collins a Christmas card and note of thanks. Collins replied with a graceful letter, which Kashiwagi said, "reveals so much of the character of this great man." Kashiwagi said later that he valued the letter "more than anything" he had, more even than the twenty-thousand-dollar reparations check he had received from the government in the early 1990s. In 1967, Karen Kimura, a Los Angeles high school student who was writing a term paper on the wartime removal and incarceration, wrote Collins, asking for his help on her project. He replied with a long letter, which among other things, emphasized that the government established "concentration camps," not "relocation centers." Kimura thanked him for his assistance and reported that she received an A on the assignment. In fact, so many of her teachers and friends wanted to read the paper, that she edited and rewrote it for what amounted to local publication.

Collins was particularly generous with his time and resources in assisting scholars and writers. He made himself available for interviews, either in person or by phone or mail. He also allowed scholars to examine his office files. Among those who took advantage of his generosity and eventually published noteworthy works were sociologists Dorothy Swaine Thomas and Richard Nishimoto, activists Audrie Girdner and Anne Loftis, journalists Bill Hosokawa and Rex Gunn, and historian Donald Collins. Wayne Collins, of course, was not always happy with the results. He was especially dismissive of Hosokawa's books, while he complimented the work of Thomas and Nishimoto.

Of all the writers and scholars with whom he worked, Collins probably established the closest bonds with Michi Nishiura Weglyn. Born in Stockton in 1926, Weglyn spent most of World War II in the Gila River camp in Arizona. After the war, she moved to

New York and became a successful costume designer for Broadway productions, New York nightclubs, and network television shows. She married a Jewish refugee from Nazi Germany, and with his support in the late sixties, began research on a critical history of the government's wartime treatment of the Nikkei. She visited Collins in San Francisco, interviewed him, and made extensive use of his files. The two became friends and kept up an active correspondence. Unfortunately, her book, *Years of Infamy*, was not published until 1975, a few months after Collins's death. He was never able to read the work, which came to be known as "the bible of the reparations movement." Weglyn dedicated the book to Collins, who she said, "lives in the memory of thousands who were beneficiaries of his fierce dedication to justice." Both Hiroshi Kashiwagi and Minoru Kiyota also dedicated their published memoirs to the memory of Wayne Collins.

Collins never retired, continuing to work out of his office in the Mills Tower. But his law practice gradually declined. His son reports that during the last year of his life, the practice earned less than three thousand dollars. However, in the summer of 1974, Collins still traveled to Hong Kong on business. On July 16, on his way home in a Pan Am jet high over the Pacific, he suffered a fatal heart attack. Unfortunately, the seventy-four-year-old attorney died surrounded by fellow passengers rather than by family and friends. The *San Francisco Examiner* reported that the city had lost a "defender of lost causes and a barrister for the forlorn." The *Chronicle* quoted Tex Nakamura as saying that Collins had been "the greatest American friend of the Japanese Americans."

In the summer of 1975, about a year after Wayne Collins's death, Iva Toguri D'Aquino returned to San Francisco for the first time in several years. She came to meet with Clifford Uyeda, who was chairing a committee of people trying to clear her name. According to Uyeda, "she did not say one word about her own ordeal. She was crusading for the memory of the elder Collins." Perhaps being back in San Francisco, Iva was especially conscious of the passing of the man who had played such an important role in her life. "There are Nisei who owe their success if not their lives to Mr. Collins," she said. "They wouldn't be where they are now if it wasn't for Mr. Collins."

Tex Nakamura believed that at the end of his life, Collins still took personally his losses in the cases of Fred Korematsu and Iva Toguri D'Aquino. But those cases weren't over. In the decade following Collins's passing, Iva won her pardon and Fred had his conviction overturned. Although Wayne Collins was not alive to celebrate these victories, they are nonetheless very much a part of the story of his life and legacy.

CHAPTER 9

VICTORIES

Although Clifford Uyeda was born of Japanese immigrant parents in Olympia, Washington, in 1917, he never experienced life in a WRA camp. Instead, he spent World War II obtaining his medical degree at Tulane University in New Orleans. In 1949, while the Tokyo Rose trial slowly proceeded in San Francisco, Uyeda was finishing his residency at Massachusetts General Hospital in Boston. He then served as an air force doctor during the Korean War. Returning to civilian life in 1953, he settled in San Francisco, becoming a pediatrician at Kaiser Permanente Hospital. He was active in community affairs, serving as president of the local chapter of the JACL in the early sixties. He became a controversial figure in San Francisco public life, criticizing the African American Civil Rights Movement for its mass demonstrations and acts of civil disobedience. Yet Uyeda was also a member of a new, activist generation of JACL leaders, who supported the establishment of Asian American studies programs at colleges and universities and campaigned for the redress movement that eventually won monetary reparations for the victims of wartime incarceration.

In 1973, Uyeda met John Hada, a retired Nisei army officer who was studying for a master's degree in history at the University of San Francisco. Hada's thesis was on the Tokyo Rose case, and it was through Hada that Uyeda first became familiar with the injustice suffered by Iva Toguri D'Aquino. This prompted Uyeda to organize and then chair the JACL National Committee for Iva Toguri in 1975. The dozen or so members of the committee had their sights set on winning a presidential pardon. Given the failure of previous attempts at executive action in the fifties and sixties, Uyeda believed that this time, the pardon request had to be preceded by a vigorous public relations campaign on Toguri's behalf. But it couldn't happen without Iva's permission and participation. The committee was well aware that she had summarily turned down JACL executive director Dave Ushio's offer of assistance in 1974. Uyeda believed that only a member of the Collins family could convince her of the committee's good faith. Since Wayne Collins was gone, Uyeda decided to approach Collins's son, Wayne Merrill Collins.

Wayne Merrill had become a member of the California Bar in 1973. After Wayne senior's death the following year, the younger Collins took over what was left of his father's law practice and moved into the old office in the Mills Building. It was there, in a room filled with files of old cases, and decorated with Japanese art purchased long ago from Senri Nao, that Clifford Uyeda first met with Wayne Merrill Collins. In spite of the sometimes difficult personal relationship between father and son, the younger Collins was proud and protective of Wayne senior's professional legacy. Wayne Merrill had also inherited his father's deep skepticism about the motives of the JACL. As Uyeda wrote, "the JACL has never been a respected name in the Collins family." The first meeting was tense, but eventually Collins became convinced of Uyeda's sincerity. He agreed to intercede on the committee's behalf with Toguri. In so doing, Wayne Merrill Collins effectively activated the campaign that was to lead to the pardon of "Tokyo Rose." That pardon was in a very real sense a posthumous victory for his father.

In August of 1975, when Iva Toguri D'Aquino came to San Francisco to meet with Uyeda at the JACL office, the younger Collins accompanied her. She had first known him as an eleven-year-old boy, but now nearly twenty years later, he had taken his father's place as her attorney. Wayne Merrill was slender like Wayne senior, but far taller. Uyeda noted how physically small Iva appeared alongside the lanky Collins. But her personality was something else. Uyeda explained that, "Iva Toguri was a dynamic individual with incredible character....She had not been broken by her ordeal." In January 1976, Iva returned to San Francisco to meet with the entire committee in what was as much a social gathering as a business session. Again she dominated the room, making a strong impression on the committee members. Before the evening meeting, Toguri and Wayne Merrill went to dinner at a Fisherman's Wharf restaurant with Uyeda and his wife Helen. Uyeda remembered that Iva ordered Dungeness crab, her personal favorite. The dinners with the Uyedas and Wayne Merrill at Fisherman's Wharf became a ritual whenever Iva was in town, and if crab was in season, that's what she ordered.

To spread its message, the committee published a pamphlet, *Iva Toguri (d'Aquino): Victim of a Legend*. The pamphlet told Toguri's story, describing her as "a victim of a World War II fantasy...a casualty of the prejudice, stereotypes, and social mores of that era." Iva Toguri had "survived harassment by the Japanese government only to be consumed by a fictitious image created by American soldiers." The committee distributed the publication to all JACL local chapters, but it was a hard sell for some JACL members. Even though the organization had officially resolved to assist Toguri, many Nisei still considered her "Tokyo Rose." Only 16 of the 106 JACL chapters made financial contributions to the campaign. While two Japanese American Veterans of Foreign Wars posts supported Iva's cause, the 1976 convention of veterans of the all-Nisei 442nd Regimental Combat Team refused to take a position on the issue.

The campaign did win crucial support in the broader community. The California State Legislature, along with the city governments of San Francisco, Los Angeles, San Jose, and Honolulu, passed resolutions of support. Several prominent newspapers, including the *San Francisco Chronicle*, the *Wall Street Journal*, and the *Denver Post*, published sympathetic articles and editorials. The *San Francisco Examiner* had a piece featuring Wayne Merrill making the case for Iva's pardon. It included a picture of him in his Mills Building office surrounded by the files of his father's Nikkei cases. But no newspaper coverage was more important than that of Toguri's hometown paper, the *Chicago Tribune*. As we have seen, in March 1976, the *Tribune* published a bombshell from its Tokyo correspondent, quoting two key government witnesses as saying that they had lied in court when they testified against Iva twenty-seven years earlier. The fact that their false testimony had come under pressure from government agents and prosecutors was not entirely shocking to readers who had recently been through the Watergate scandal. In 1976, many Americans were willing to believe the worst about their public officials.

Walter Cronkite's CBS evening news picked up the story. Even more important, in April, the network's *60 Minutes*, one of the nation's highest-rated television programs, featured a twenty-minute segment on the case. Under the sympathetic questioning of newsman Morley Safer, Toguri told her story in calm, articulate fashion. She came across not so much as a victim, but as someone very much in charge of her life and her campaign for justice. Safer observed that back in 1949, "It was not Iva on trial, it was Tokyo Rose." The program also featured former jury foreman John Mann, who said "there have been very few months since the trial that I did not think of her and think that she was not guilty."

The reaction was not entirely positive. Toguri got so much hate mail that she stopped opening envelopes delivered to her home and business. Only later did she realize that many of the unopened letters contained messages of support and even financial contributions. In fact, the committee was convinced that the campaign was succeeding, creating growing public support for the pardon. Some members felt they should strike while the iron was hot and immediately apply for the pardon in the wake of the *60 Minutes* broadcast.

But Wayne Merrill Collins argued that they should wait until the outcome of the 1976 presidential election between President Gerald Ford and challenger Jimmy Carter. That way the issue would not become a part of the divisive electoral campaign. The committee accepted Collins's strategy, and the application was not filed until November 17, 1976. By then, Ford had lost the election, and as a lame-duck president, he had little to lose politically by granting the pardon. Toguri and Collins announced the application at a well-attended press conference in front of the same San Francisco federal courthouse where Iva had been convicted twenty-seven years before.

By then, the pardon had the influential support of S. I. Hayakawa, the newly elected United States senator from California.

An academic, Hayakawa had spent World War II teaching English in Chicago, and like Clifford Uyeda, he had avoided incarceration in WRA camps. He became a professor at San Francisco State in 1955, establishing a reputation as a well regarded semanticist and political liberal. But during the 1968 student strike on the San Francisco State campus, Hayakawa became the university's president and a conservative hero for his outspoken opposition to the strikers. In 1976, he became a US senator, running as a conservative Republican. His father and Iva's father had been friends as young Japanese immigrants in British Columbia, and in San Francisco, Professor Hayakawa had come to know Clifford Uyeda. In January 1977, Hayakawa agreed to privately lobby fellow Republican Gerald Ford on Toguri's behalf.

Nevertheless, as Ford's term wound down with no word on the pardon, Toguri and her allies became increasingly pessimistic. Then on January 17, two days before the end of the Ford administration, CBS reported a rumor that the pardon was forthcoming. Collins and Uyeda attempted to confirm the report with only partial success. On January 19, Ford's last day in office, Uyeda was on the phone long distance with Toguri, who was at her store in Chicago. She asked to be excused for a moment, and then came back on the line, and said, "It's true." She had just heard from Washington: the president had granted her pardon. President Ford's action was the first full and unconditional pardon given to someone convicted of treason. It restored Iva Toguri D'Aquino's rights of citizenship. For the first time since 1942, she could obtain an American passport and vote in an American election. She continued to manage the family's Chicago store for many years and died in 2006, at the age of ninety.

When he had first heard the news on the phone with Iva, Clifford Uyeda said that he believed "if Wayne Mortimer Collins and Theodore Tamba [who died in 1973] were still alive...how they would have rejoiced this day." Uyeda recalled that when no one else would take her case, "Collins became Iva Toguri's protector" and remained "her champion for over a quarter of a century." Other than Iva herself, Uyeda believed the people most responsible for her victory were "Wayne Mortimer Collins and his son Wayne Merrill Collins."

The pardon was the elder Collins's first posthumous victory. He had campaigned for Iva's pardon for more than a quarter century, and the efforts of his son, the committee, and Iva herself finally accomplished it two and a half years after his death. His second posthumous victory came in 1983.

As we saw in chapter 3, in 1981 legal scholar Peter Irons and researcher Aiko Herzig-Yoshinaga had discovered significant irregularities in the Justice Department's prosecution of the *Korematsu* case during the 1940s. At the direction of Solicitor General Charles Fahy, department lawyers did not inform the court that General DeWitt's *Final Report* had been altered and that investigations of the FBI and Office of Naval Intelligence had concluded that the mass incarceration was unnecessary. This evidence would have provided solid support for Wayne Collins's argument that the executive order and subsequent military proclamations were unconstitutional because they had no reasonable national security purpose and were instead motivated by racism and political expediency.

Irons shared his discoveries with a team of primarily Sansei (third-generation Japanese American) lawyers led by San Francisco attorney Dale Minami, and including Don Tamaki and Lorraine

Bannai. With Irons's assistance, the lawyers filed an appeal in the federal district court in San Francisco, requesting reversal of Fred Korematsu's conviction for violating Public Law 503, which made it a crime to disobey Executive Order 9066 and its implementation decrees. Minami's team appealed on the basis of the little known legal doctrine of coram nobis, which allows for overturning guilty verdicts in cases when serious prosecutorial misconduct results in fundamental injustice. The government offered a presidential pardon, but Korematsu's lawyers insisted on petitioning the judge to reopen the case and reconsider the verdict.

On November 10, 1983, Federal District Judge Marilyn Hall Patel granted Korematsu's motion and overturned his conviction. Patel found that the government's arguments supporting the executive order, the military decrees, and Public Law 503 were based on "unsubstantiated facts, distortions and representations of at least one military commander, whose views were seriously infected by racism." In her written opinion, Judge Patel found that in the case against Korematsu, "the government deliberately omitted relevant information and provided misleading information in papers before the court." After eliminating the government's false arguments and misleading evidence, what Judge Patel was left with was Wayne Collins's original constitutional objection to the prosecution and conviction of Fred Korematsu.

For much of the postwar era, Fred Korematsu had kept a low profile and avoided the subject of his criminal conviction. His daughter Karen first heard of the case in a school classroom rather than from her father. But the successful coram nobis action gave Korematsu new confidence and energy. In spite of his natural shyness, he became an effective advocate for the cause of civil rights and civil liberties. In 1998, President Bill Clinton awarded Korematsu the Presidential Medal of Freedom. Clinton said that "in the long history of our country's constant search for justice, some names stand for millions of souls....To that distinguished list, today we add the name of Fred Korematsu." In the wake of 9/11, Fred spoke out against anti-Muslim prejudice. After his death in 2006, the California legislature established January 30 as the Fred Korematsu Day of Civil Liberties and the Constitution.

Some of the Sansei attorneys representing Fred Korematsu in 1983 were also involved in the coram nobis proceedings in Seattle that resulted in overturning the conviction of Gordon Hirabayashi for violating Public Law 503. Similar action regarding the case of Minoru Yasui in Portland failed only because of Yasui's death before the completion of the legal process. (In the 1940s, Wayne Collins had written amicus briefs in these cases.) The 1980s coram nobis cases were part of a growing activist trend in the Japanese American community that included the redress movement. Indeed, by the early eighties, redress was easily the most important political cause within the community.

At a JACL convention in 1970, Edison Uno, who pioneered much of the new Nisei activism during the seventies, formally introduced the concept of redress in the form of monetary reparations for victims of Executive Order 9066. By the time that Clifford Uyeda was elected JACL president in 1978, the redress movement was well under way, and Uyeda made it central to his presidency. He appointed John Tateishi chair of an active JACL redress committee. Uyeda attended the 1980 ceremony at which President Jimmy Carter signed legislation establishing the Federal Commission on Wartime Relocation and Internment of Civilians. In 1981, the commission, whose nine members were chosen by Congress and the president, held hearings in eleven cities and heard from more than seven hundred and fifty witnesses. The majority of the witnesses were sympathetic to the concept of redress, but some, like former assistant secretary of war John J. McCloy, opposed reparations and defended the wartime incarceration.

One of the witnesses who supported redress was Edward Ennis. He had gone from opposing Executive Order 9066 to loyally defending the president's policy, then entering into private discussions with the national ACLU regarding suppressed evidence. Yet Ennis subsequently took a hard-line stance against the Tule Lake renunciants, strongly advocating their deportation. Over the years, no one had been on more different and contradictory sides of the issues of wartime removal, incarceration, and deportation than Edward Ennis.

After leaving the Justice Department in 1946, Ennis briefly served as counsel for the JACL. He was ACLU chief national counsel from 1955 to 1969 and president of the organization from 1967 to 1977. Testifying in support of redress before the federal commission in 1981, Ennis admitted "I did represent the defendant government in evacuation actions and indeed wrote the briefs, argued the cases in the lower courts, and wrote briefs for the Solicitor General for the Supreme Court of the United States. I should confess that." Looking back, Ennis said, "I don't know why I didn't resign." Had Wayne Collins still been alive, it's unlikely he would have had much sympathy for Edward Ennis. Unlike Ennis, Collins had no divided loyalties. His allegiance was always to his Nikkei clients and to what he understood to be the principles of the United States Constitution.

The commission issued its final report in 1982. The nine members unanimously concluded that the policy of removal and incarceration was unnecessary, unconstitutional, and motivated by racism and political expediency. The 1983 report paved the way for the eventual passage of the Civil Liberties Act of 1988. The measure received substantial bipartisan congressional support and was signed into law by President Ronald Reagan. It formally apologized for Executive Order 9066 and the policies it engendered and provided for a payment of twenty thousand dollars to each of the approximately sixty thousand former camp prisoners who were still living. The measure also included individual payments of five thousand dollars to Alaska natives the government had forcibly removed from their island homes during the war. The Civil Liberties Act represented a substantial victory for the redress movement and the new generation of Nikkei leaders, including Clifford Uyeda. It also represented the triumph of the values and spirit that motivated the long legal battles of Wayne Collins.

CHAPTER 10

PRECEDENT

Wayne Collins often told Iva Toguri D'Aquino, "At least you've led an eventful life full of excitements, though mostly painful. The rest of us had a dull and monotonous life." No matter how "dull and monotonous" Collins believed his own life to be, he certainly suffered pain—the early deaths of his father and wife, for example. His many frustrations and grudges sometimes led to volatile expressions of anger that threatened personal and family relationships. But there were also lifelong friendships and family ties that survived the difficult times.

Collins's legal career included many defeats—the initial devastating losses in the *Korematsu* and Tokyo Rose cases, to name just two. But there were also high points. Although raised in an institution for poor and troubled boys and forced to work his way through night school to become a lawyer, Collins appeared before the US Supreme Court and stood toe-to-toe with members of the nation's legal establishment. He prevailed in conflicts with the national ACLU and JACL, defended the rights of Japanese Peruvians, and forced the WRA to close the Tule Lake stockade. He outlasted the US government to preserve the rights and liberties of thousands of renunciants. For the legal battles he fought, including some of those he lost, Collins won the deep gratitude and respect of many

Nikkei. Even the JACL eventually recognized his great contributions to cause of civil rights and civil liberties.

The Civil Liberties Act of 1988 included language that said Executive Order 9066 and the terrible policies it initiated were the product "of race prejudice, war hysteria, and a failure of political leadership." That was essentially the argument that Wayne Collins had made in his first brief in the *Korematsu* case in 1942. In the ensuing decades, he never wavered, never compromised. Forty-six years later, with passage of the Civil Liberties Act, the Congress, the president, and presumably the nation, finally caught up with him. It was as if they were saying, "Mr. Collins, it turns out that you were right all the time." It would be a national tragedy if in our own era, reacting to the rhetoric of demagogues and the fears engendered by terrorism and significant economic and demographic change, Americans were to return to something like the prejudices of the 1940s and come to view Executive Order 9066 as a positive precedent.

Back in 1942, Assistant Secretary of War John J. McCloy had said that the Constitution "was just a scrap of paper." Collins never agreed and worked most of his professional life to transform the noble words of the Constitution into practical reality, even to the point of challenging the authority of an immensely popular and powerful president of the United States during a time of war. In the long run, Wayne Collins's interpretation of the Constitution prevailed, not only over that of John J. McCloy, but over that of Franklin D. Roosevelt, as well. Collins's legal battles helped individual clients and also helped the Nikkei as an oppressed ethnic group to gain the space, time, and support necessary to organize its own powerful campaigns against unconstitutional injustice. The long and ultimately successful fight to make constitutional protections of rights and liberties something more than "just a scrap of paper" is the overriding legacy of Wayne Mortimer Collins, the vital precedent he established for us and for future generations.

SOURCES

CHAPTER 1

Hiroshi Kashiwagi's memoir is *Swimming in the American: A Memoir and Selected Writings* (2005). Wayne Collins's role in defending Hiroshi Kashiwagi and other renunciants is covered in Donald E. Collins, *Native American Aliens: Disloyalty and the Renunciation of Citizenship by Japanese Americans during World War II* (1985). For general coverage and interpretation of the Asian American experience in California and the United States, see Sucheng Chan, *Asian Californians* (1991) and Ronald Takaki, *A Different Mirror: A History of Multicultural America* (1993). *Personal Justice Denied: Report of the Commission on Wartime Relocation and Internment of Civilians* (1982) is a government commission investigation and interpretation of Executive Order 9066 and the subsequent Nikkei removal and incarceration.

CHAPTER 2

Much of the material in this chapter is based on information in the Wayne M. Collins Papers, archived in The Bancroft Library, University of California, Berkeley (Wayne M. Collins Papers, BANC MSS 78/177c). For information about the contents of the collection, see *Guide to the Wayne M. Collins Papers* at The Bancroft Library. Other valuable sources were three interviews I conducted with his son, Wayne Merrill Collins, in 2016 and 2017. Obituaries, marriage notices, et cetera, in local newspapers, particularly the *San Francisco Chronicle* and the *San Francisco Examiner*, were also helpful. Greg Robinson and Brian Niiya have written a useful summary of Collins's life in the online *Densho Encyclopedia* (encyclopedia .densho.org). The archives of the Northern California branch of the American Civil Liberties Union are in the library of the California Historical Society in San Francisco (ACLU MS 3580). Two valuable works on the relationship between the national ACLU and the Northern California branch are Judy Kutulas, *The American Civil Liberties Union and the Making of Modern Liberalism, 1930–1960* (2006) and "In Quest of Autonomy: The Northern California Affiliate of the American Civil Liberties Union and World War II," *Pacific Historical Review* (May 1998). Another useful source is Elaine Elinson and Stan Yogi, *Wherever There's a Fight: How Runaway Slaves, Suffragists, Immigrants, Strikers, and Poets Shaped Civil Liberties in California* (2009).

CHAPTER 3

Peter Irons's study and analysis of the *Korematsu* case is *Justice at War: The Story of the Japanese American Interment Cases* (1983). For a critical review of Irons's work, see Neil Gotanda, "'Other Non-Whites' in American Legal History: A Review Essay on *Justice at War*," *Journal of Gender, Race, and Justice* (2009–2010). Coverage of the case and Wayne Collins's role are included in Roger Daniels, *The Japanese American Cases: The Rule of Law in Time of War* (2013), and Lorraine K. Bannai, *Enduring Conviction: Fred Korematsu and His Quest for Justice* (2015). The conflicts between the national ACLU office and the Northern California branch are documented in the Wayne M. Collins Papers (previously cited) and the archives of the Northern California branch of the ACLU (previously cited). These issues are also discussed in the previously cited works of Judy Kutulas and of Elaine Elinson and Stan Yogi. Greg Robinson discusses the importance of the *Korematsu* decision in *After Camp: Portraits in Midcentury Japanese American Life and Politics* (2012).

The citation for the decision in the *Korematsu* case, including con-
curring and dissenting opinions, is *Korematsu v. the United States*,
323 U.S. 214 (1944).

CHAPTER 4

Eugene V. Rostow's article, "The Japanese American Cases: A
Disaster" appeared in the *Yale Law Journal* (1945). Barbara Takei
discusses conditions at Tule Lake in "Legalizing Detention: Seg-
regated Japanese Americans and the Justice Department's Renunciation Program," in *Discover Nikkei* online (discovernikkei.org,
March 15–May 10, 2015). Also see Barbara Takei and Judy Tachibana, *Tule Lake Revisited: A Brief History and Guide to the Tule Lake
Internment Camp Site* (2001), and Dorothy Swaine Thomas and
Richard S. Nishimoto, *The Spoilage* (1946) and *The Salvage* (1952).
Dillon Myer discusses his perspective on the incarceration and the
specific conditions at Tule Lake in his oral history, *Autobiography
of Dillon S. Myer*, The Bancroft Library (BANC MSS 71/862,
1971), and in his memoir, *Uprooted Americans: The Japanese Amer-
icans and the War Relocation Authority during World War II* (1971).
Richard Drinnon's biography of Myer, *Keeper of the Concentration
Camps: Dillon S. Myer and American Racism* (1987) is highly critical of Myer and highly complimentary of Wayne Collins. The Fair
Play Committee is covered in Charles Wollenberg, "'Dear Earl':
The Fair Play Committee, Earl Warren, and Japanese Internment,"
California History (Winter 2012). Bill Hosokawa's *JACL in Quest
of Justice* (1980) is an interpretation of the Japanese American Cit-
izens League's history. Ernest Besig's experience at Tule Lake is
documented in the archives of the Northern California branch of
the ACLU (previously cited) and discussed in the works of Judy
Kutulas (also previously cited). Wayne Collins's opposition to the
Tule Lake stockade is discussed in the Wayne M. Collins Papers

(previously cited), Donald E. Collins, *Native American Aliens* (also previously cited), and Michi Nishiura Weglyn, *Years of Infamy: The Untold Story of America's Concentration Camps* (1976).

CHAPTER 5

The Justice Department's advocacy of Public Law 405 is discussed in John Christgau, "Collins versus the World: The Fight to Restore Citizenship to Japanese American Renunciants of World War II," *Pacific Historical Review* (February 1985), Ellen Clare Kennedy, "The Japanese-American Renunciants: Due Process and the Danger of Making Laws during Times of Fear," Japanese Policy Research Institute (October 2006), and Donald E. Collins (previously cited). The previously cited works of Barbara Takei and Judy Tachibana, and Dorothy Swaine Thomas and Richard S. Nishimoto discuss the conditions at Tule Lake and the impact of Public Law 405 on people incarcerated there. The Wayne M. Collins Papers (previously cited) and the archives of the Northern California branch of the American Civil Liberties Union (previously cited) contain many letters between renunciants and Justice Department lawyers. Hiroshi Kashiwagi's memoir (previously cited) and Minoru Kiyota, *Beyond Loyalty: The Story of a Kibei* (1997) also describe the ordeal of Tule Lake renunciants. Wayne Collins's papers include coverage of his activity on behalf of the renunciants and extensive communications between him and the Tule Lake Defense Committee. These subjects are also covered in the previously cited works of Michi Weglyn, Donald Collins, and John Christgau. Tetsujiro "Tex" Nakamura's 2009 interview appears in the Densho Digital Repository (archive.densho.org). Judge Lewis E. Goodman's background is covered in Eric L. Muller, *Free to Die For Their Country: The Story of the Japanese American Draft Resisters in World War II* (2001) and Richard Cahan, Pia Hinckle, and Jessica Royer Ocken,

The Court That Tamed the West: From the Gold Rush to the Tech Boom (2013). The Wayne M. Collins papers include a copy of Goodman's decision in the *Abo* case.

CHAPTER 6

A. L. Wirin's correspondence with Wayne Collins and Ernest Besig appears in the Wayne M. Collins Papers (previously cited). Greg Robinson and Brian Niiya cover Wirin's background in the online *Densho Encyclopedia* (previously cited). Collins's conflict with Wirin is discussed in Donald E. Collins (previously cited) and Judy Kutulas, "In Quest of Autonomy" (previously cited). The citation for the Ninth Circuit's decision in *Abo v. Clark* is 186 F.2d 776 (9th Cir. 1951). The Wayne M. Collins Papers contain a vast amount of material on the renunciant appeal process, including considerable correspondence regarding the Tule Lake Defense Committee. Tex Nakamura's previously cited interview appears in the Densho Digital Repository. For background of the Wada family, see Yori Wada's oral history at The Bancroft Library, "Working for Youth and Social Justice: The YMCA, the University of California, and the Stulsaft Foundation" (BANC MSS 92/770c, 1991). Theodore Tamba's "The Peruvian Japanese" is part of the material on the Japanese Peruvian controversy in the Wayne M. Collins Papers. The Japanese Peruvian issue is also discussed in Audrie Girdner and Anne Loftis, *The Great Betrayal: The Evacuation of the Japanese-Americans during World War II* (1969), and in the previously cited work by Elaine Elinson and Stan Yogi. Department of Justice press releases and statements on the renunciant issue, including a report on the1959 ceremony in Washington, DC, are included in the Wayne M. Collins Papers. The papers also include a copy of Collins's 1968 statement announcing the end of the renunciant cases.

CHAPTER 7

The Tokyo Rose case is covered in Yasuhide Kawashima, *The Tokyo Rose Case: Treason on Trial* (2013), Russell Warren Howe, *The Hunt for "Tokyo Rose"* (1990), and Stanley I. Kutler, "Forging a Legend: The Treason of 'Tokyo Rose,'" in Charles J. McClain, ed., *The Mass Internment of Japanese Americans and the Quest for Legal Redress* (1994). Rex Gunn covered the 1949 trial as a journalist, and interviewed Wayne Collins, Iva Toguri D'Aquino, and many of the other participants. His personal experience with the case is reflected in his *They Called Her Tokyo Rose* (1977). Dean Lipton also knew both Collins and Toguri and wrote sympathetically of them in "Wayne M. Collins and the Case of 'Tokyo Rose,'" *Journal of Contemporary Studies* (Fall/Winter 1985). Collins's associate in the case, George Olshausen, discussed the public's misconceptions in "Tokyo Rose: Folklore and Justice," *City Lights* (July 1952). Another participant in the case, Tex Nakamura, discussed the trial in his previously cited Densho Repository interview. Wayne Merrill Collins included his memories of Toguri in his previously cited interviews with the author. The eight counts in the government's indictment are listed in Clifford I. Uyeda, *A Final Report and Review: The Japanese American Citizens League National Committee for Iva Toguri* (1980). The trial and its aftermath received substantial coverage in the national and regional media, particularly the *San Francisco Chronicle*, *Oakland Tribune*, and *San Francisco Examiner*. The admission of false testimony appears in the *Chicago Tribune* (March 22, 1976).

CHAPTER 8

The catalogue for the 1972 California Historical Society exhibit is Maisie and Richard Conrat, *Executive Order 9066: The Internment of 110,000 Japanese Americans* (1972). Edison Uno's letter is in the

office files of the California Historical Society, San Francisco. Dean
Lipton's comments are from his previously cited "Wayne M. Collins and the Case of 'Tokyo Rose.'" The previously cited Wayne M.
Collins Papers include letters on family matters and on Collins's
criticisms of the JACL and ACLU. The Wayne M. Collins Papers
also include correspondence with renunciants and with Karen
Kimura, the Los Angeles high school student. The works of Dorothy Swaine Thomas and Richard Nishimoto, Audrei Girdner and
Anne Loftis, Bill Hosokawa, Rex Gunn, and Donald Collins have
all been previously cited. Michi Weglyn's influential work is *Years of
Infamy* (previously cited). Clifford Uyeda's *Final Report and Review*
and the memoirs of Hiroshi Kashiwagi and Minoru Kiyota have
also been previously cited. The *San Francisco Chronicle* and the *San
Francisco Examiner* published obituaries for Wayne Collins on July
18, 1974.

CHAPTERS 9 AND 10

Greg Robinson summarizes Clifford Uyeda's background in the
online *Densho Encyclopedia* (previously cited). Uyeda's account
of the Toguri pardon campaign is covered in *A Final Report and
Review* (previously cited), and "The Pardoning of 'Tokyo Rose': A
Report on the Restoration of American Citizenship to Iva Toguri,"
in Charles McClain, ed., *The Mass Internment of Japanese Americans
and the Quest for Legal Redress* (1994). Wayne Merrill Collins commented on the campaign in his previously cited interviews with the
author. The JACL National Committee for Iva Toguri pamphlet on
the case was *Iva Toguri (d'Aquino): Victim of a Legend* (1975). Dean
Lipton knew both Wayne Collins and Iva Toguri and covered the
pardon campaign in "Wayne M. Collins and the Case of 'Tokyo
Rose'" (previously cited). Wayne Merrill Collins's interview with
the *San Francisco Examiner* appeared on February 23, 1976. The

Chicago Tribune article on the false testimony of witnesses appeared on March 22, 1976 (previously cited). The 1976 *60 Minutes* broadcast on the case can be viewed on YouTube (https://www.youtube.com/watch?v=olzvi-qRqa0, accessed October 1, 2014). For background on Hayakawa, see Gerald W. Haslam and Janice E. Haslam, *In Thought and Action: The Enigmatic Life of S. I. Hayakawa* (2011). The effort to overturn Fred Korematsu's conviction is covered in Lorraine K. Bannai, *Enduring Conviction* (previously cited). Also see Peter Irons, *Justice at War* (previously cited) and "Fancy Dancing at the Marble Palace," in Charles McClain, ed., *The Mass Internment of Japanese Americans and the Quest for Legal Redress* (1994). The report of the Commission on Wartime Relocation and Internment of Civilians, *Personal Justice Denied*, was published in 1982.

ABOUT THE AUTHOR

Charles Wollenberg, former chair of social sciences and professor of history at Berkeley City College, is coeditor, with Marcia A. Eymann, of *What's Going On?: California and the Vietnam Era* (University of California Press, 2004) and author of *Marinship at War: Shipbuilding and Social Change in Wartime Sausalito* (Western Heritage, 1990) and *Berkeley: A City in History* (University of California Press, 2008).

ABOUT THE CALIFORNIA HISTORICAL SOCIETY BOOK AWARD

In 2013, after a twenty-year collaboration and with a shared commitment to finding new and inclusive ways to explore California's history, the California Historical Society and Heyday established the California Historical Society Book Award as a way of inviting new voices and viewpoints into the conversation. Each year we bring together a jury of noted historians, scholars, and publishing experts to award a book-length manuscript that makes an important contribution both to scholarship and to the greater community by deepening public understanding of some aspect of California history.

For more information, visit www.heydaybooks.com/chsbookaward or http://www.californiahistoricalsociety.org/publications/book_award.html.

CALIFORNIA
HISTORICAL
SOCIETY since 1871

ABOUT THE CALIFORNIA HISTORICAL SOCIETY

Founded in 1871, the California Historical Society (CHS) is a nonprofit organization with a mission to inspire and empower people to make California's richly diverse past a meaningful part of their contemporary lives.

PUBLIC ENGAGEMENT

Through high-quality public history exhibitions, public programs, research, preservation, advocacy, and digital storytelling, CHS keeps history alive through extensive public engagement. In opening the very heart of the organization—our vast and diverse collection—to ever wider audiences, we invite meaning, encourage exchange, and enrich understanding.

CHS COLLECTIONS

CHS holds one of the state's top historical collections, revealing California's social, cultural, economic, and political history and development—including some of the most cherished and valuable documents and images of California's past. From our headquarters in San Francisco to the University of Southern California and the

Autry National Center in Los Angeles, we hold millions of items in trust for the people of California.

LIBRARY AND RESEARCH

Open to the public and free of charge, our North Baker Research Library is a place where researchers literally hold history in their hands. Whether you're a scholar or are simply interested in learning about the history of your neighborhood, city, or community, you have hands-on access to the rich history of our state.

PUBLICATIONS

From our first book publication in 1874, to our ninety-year history as publisher of the *California History* journal, to the establishment of the annual California Historical Society Book Award in 2013, CHS publications examine the ongoing dialogue between the past and the present. Our print and digital publications reach beyond purely historical narrative to connect Californians to their state, region, nation, and the world in innovative and thought-provoking ways.

SUPPORT

Over the years, the generosity and commitment of foundations, corporations, cultural and educational institutions, and private donors and members have supported CHS's work throughout the state.

LEARN MORE

www.californiahistoricalsociety.com

HEYDAY
into California

ABOUT HEYDAY

Heyday is an independent, nonprofit publisher and unique cultural institution. We promote widespread awareness and celebration of California's many cultures, landscapes, and boundary-breaking ideas. Through our well-crafted books, public events, and innovative outreach programs we are building a vibrant community of readers, writers, and thinkers.

THANK YOU

It takes the collective effort of many to create a thriving literary culture. We are thankful to all the thoughtful people we have the privilege to engage with. Cheers to our writers, artists, editors, storytellers, designers, printers, bookstores, critics, cultural organizations, readers, and book lovers everywhere!

We are especially grateful for the generous funding we've received for our publications and programs during the past year from foundations and hundreds of individual donors. Major supporters include:

Anonymous (5); John Atwood, in memory of Jeanne Carevic; Judith and Phillip Auth; Judy Avery; Carroll Ballard and Christina

Lüscher-Ballard; Richard and Rickie Ann Baum; BayTree Fund; Robert Joseph Bell and Gwendolyn Wynne; Jean and Fred Berensmeier; Joan Berman; Nancy Bertelsen; Joan Bingham; Edwin Blue; Teresa Book and Steve Wax, in memory of Saul Alinsky; Beatrice Bowles; Philip and Jamie Bowles, in memory of Mike McCone; Peter Boyer and Terry Gamble Boyer; John Briscoe; California State Library; The Campbell Foundation; The Christensen Fund; The City of Berkeley; Lawrence Crooks; H. Dwight Damon, in memory of Jim Houston; Bruce De Benedictis and Caroline Kim; Meera Desai; Chris Desser and Kirk Marckwald; Frances Dinkelspiel and Gary Wayne; Steven Dinkelspiel; Tim Disney; Patricia Dixon; Michael Eaton and Charity Kenyon; Gayle Embrey; Richard and Gretchen Evans; Federated Indians of Graton Rancheria; Megan Fletcher, in honor of J.K. Dineen; Don and Dale Franzen; John Gage and Linda Schacht; Patrick Golden and Susan Overhauser; Nicola Gordon; Wanda Lee Graves and Stephen Duscha; Whitney Green; Walter & Elise Haas Fund; Coke and James Hallowell; Anthea Hartig and John Swiecki; Lizbeth Hasse; Hearst Corporation; Anthony Heilbut; James Hirst; Adam and Arlie Hochschild; Nettie Hoge; Michael Horn, in memory of Gary Horn; Humboldt Area Foundation; Claudia Jurmain; Kalliopeia Foundation; Marty Krasney, in honor of Gary Snyder; Guy Lampard and Suzanne Badenhoop; Christine Leefeldt, in memory of Ernest "Chick" Callenbach; Thomas Lockard and Alix Marduel; David Loeb; Judith Lowry-Croul and Brad Croul; Susan Lyne; Praveen Madan and Christin Evans; Joel Marcus; Malcolm and Rina Margolin; William McClung; Michael McCone; Judy Mistelske-Anklam and William Anklam; Karen and Tom Mulvaney; The Nature Conservancy; Eddie and Amy Orton, in honor of Sherry Wasserman; Susan Rosenberg; Alan Rosenus; San Manuel Band of Mission Indians; Greg Sarris; Save the Redwoods League; Peter Schrag and Patricia Ternahan; Barbara Snell, in memory of Chuck Snell; Roselyne Swig; Miye Takagi; Tappan Foundation; Michael and Shirley Traynor, in honor of the Heyday Staff; Katrina vanden Heuvel; Al Wasserman and Ann Dragoon-Wasserman; Sherry Wasserman and Clayton F. Johnson; Lucinda Watson; Peter Wiley; Mason and Wendy Willrich, in memory of Mike McCone; Mina Witteman; and Michael Zilkha.

BOARD OF DIRECTORS

Richard D. Baum (Cochair), Don Franzen, Whitney Green, Nettie Hoge (Cochair), Marty Krasney, Guy Lampard (Chair Emeritus), Ralph Lewin, Sonia Torres, Michael Traynor, and Johanna Vondeling.

GETTING INVOLVED

To learn more about our publications, events, and other ways you can participate, please visit www.heydaybooks.com.

San Francisco Chronicle photograph of Wayne Collins during the Tokyo Rose trial, 1949. Photograph by Bob Campbell. Courtesy of *San Francisco Chronicle*/Polaris.

Wayne Collins and World War I shipmates at the Kilauea volcano in Hawaii, ca. 1918–19. Collins is in the dark uniform on the right. Courtesy of The Bancroft Library, University of California, Berkeley (Portraits from the Wayne M. Collins Papers, BANC PIC 1978.156—A).

Thelma Garrison Collins with daughter Margaret, 1942. Three years later, the Collinses had a son, Wayne Merrill. Courtesy of The Bancroft Library, University of California, Berkeley (Portraits from the Wayne M. Collins Papers, BANC PIC 1978.156—A).

Wayne Collins (center) flanked by son Wayne Merrill (left) and family friend Dr. William Weiner (right) at an outing to the Broderick-Terry Duel monument, Lake Merced, San Francisco, 1960. Courtesy of The Bancroft Library, University of California, Berkeley (Portraits from the Wayne M. Collins Papers, BANC PIC 1978.156—A).

Wedding of Chiyo Nao and Yoritada Wada, 1944. Chiyo had known Wayne Collins, a family friend, all her life and served as his indispensable office secretary in the postwar years. Courtesy of Shades of San Francisco, San Francisco Public Library.

Ernest Besig, longtime executive director of the Northern California branch of the ACLU and colleague, friend, and supporter of Wayne Collins in the Korematsu and other Nikkei cases. Courtesy of the American Civil Liberties Union Foundation of Northern California.

Wayne Collins in his Mills Building office, 1942. His desktop is in its usual state of chaotic disarray. Courtesy of The Bancroft Library, University of California, Berkeley (Portraits from the Wayne M. Collins Papers, BANC PIC 1978.156—A).

Young Fred Korematsu, ca. 1941. He allowed Wayne Collins and the Northern California Branch of the ACLU to use his case to challenge the constitutionality of Executive Order 9066. Courtesy of the Fred T. Korematsu Institute.

Fred Korematsu (third from left) with his family at their East Bay nursery, ca. 1941. Courtesy of the Fred T. Korematsu Institute.

Protestors held in the Tule Lake stockade, 1944. Some of the men were imprisoned without due process for nine months. By threatening court action, Wayne Collins twice forced camp authorities to close the stockade. Photograph by R. H. Ross. Courtesy of the National Archives.

Members of the pro-Japan Hoshi Dan, held in the Tule Lake stockade before being sent to the Department of Justice internment camp for enemy aliens in Bismarck, North Dakota, June 1945. Photograph by R. H. Ross. Courtesy of the National Archives.

Young Japanese Peruvians at the Department of Justice internment camp at Crystal City, Texas, 1945. Emiko (third from left in the back row) was an American-born Nisei, probably formerly incarcerated at Tule Lake, who volunteered to teach the Peruvians English. Wayne Collins successfully defended the right of three hundred Japanese Peruvians to remain in the United States after the war. Courtesy of Densho/A. Shibayama Collection.

Tokyo Rose trial defense team, 1949. From left to right: Wayne Collins, George Olshausen, Tetsujiro ("Tex") Nakamura, Iva Toguri ("Tokyo Rose"), and Theodore Tamba. Courtesy of The Bancroft Library, University of California, Berkeley (BANC PIC 1959.010—NEG, Part 2, Box 105, 77939.16:4).

Iva Toguri, "Tokyo Rose," during her treason trial in San Francisco in 1949. Courtesy of AP Photo/ Clarence Hamm.

Ivy Toguri shortly before receiving her presidential pardon from President Ford in January 1977. Courtesy of Everett Collection Historical/Alamy Stock Photo.